An Enlightened Cheerleader

Volume 1: A Journey to Self-Mastery

Wynne Marie Lacey

BALBOA
PRESS
A DIVISION OF HAY HOUSE

Copyright © 2014 Wynne Marie Lacey.

All rights reserved. No part of this book may be used or reproduced by any means,
graphic, electronic, or mechanical, including photocopying, recording, taping or by any
information storage retrieval system without the written permission of the publisher
except in the case of brief quotations embodied in critical articles and reviews.

Assisted by Heather Ruffalo

Photo by Bill Smith

Balboa Press books may be ordered through booksellers or by contacting:

Balboa Press
A Division of Hay House
1663 Liberty Drive
Bloomington, IN 47403
www.balboapress.com
1 (877) 407-4847

Because of the dynamic nature of the Internet, any web addresses or links contained in
this book may have changed since publication and may no longer be valid. The views
expressed in this work are solely those of the author and do not necessarily reflect the
views of the publisher, and the publisher hereby disclaims any responsibility for them.

The author of this book does not dispense medical advice or prescribe the use of any
technique as a form of treatment for physical, emotional, or medical problems without the
advice of a physician, either directly or indirectly. The intent of the author is only to offer
information of a general nature to help you in your quest for emotional and spiritual well-
being. In the event you use any of the information in this book for yourself, which is your
constitutional right, the author and the publisher assume no responsibility for your actions.

Any people depicted in stock imagery provided by Thinkstock are models,
and such images are being used for illustrative purposes only.
Certain stock imagery © Thinkstock.

Printed in the United States of America.

ISBN: 978-1-4525-8932-9 (sc)
ISBN: 978-1-4525-8934-3 (hc)
ISBN: 978-1-4525-8933-6 (e)

Library of Congress Control Number: 2013923470

Balboa Press rev. date: 1/2/2014

As long as I have…
Life in my body
Love in my heart
Wisdom in my soul
Truth in my intentions
…there is reason to share

Thanks for helping me share, Heather!

CONTENTS

Chapter 1: Those Were the Days (or so I thought)............1

Chapter 2: Once a Cheerleader, Always a Cheerleader 7

Chapter 3: If You are Happy and You Know it—Savor it 19

Chapter 4: The Total Package is Only the Envelope....................31

Chapter 5: The Life Formula..43

Chapter 6: Intentions: Out with the Old, In with the New 51

Chapter 7: Energy: The Equal Playing Field................................59

Chapter 8: Matter: The Temporary Boundary........................67

Chapter 9: Be Your Own Personal Cheerleader 77

Chapter 10: Feminine Feminists 87

Chapter 11: Carpe Diem..97

Creed of An Enlightened Cheerleader 103

References 105

1

THOSE WERE THE DAYS (OR SO I THOUGHT)

The game wasn't even over when I felt my throat tighten, and it became hard to swallow. A tear escaped as I glanced and saw 2 minutes left on the clock. It hit me then that these would be my final moments as a Chicago Bulls Luvabull cheerleader in the National Basketball Association (NBA). We hadn't made it to the playoffs, and this was the last home game of the regular season. It would be my last time to dance on the Bulls' court. It would be the first time I would show any emotion other than "happy" in my uniform.

As the buzzer rang to signal the end of the game, I let out the sob that had been stuck in my throat. As I walked to center court for our traditional end of year picture, I was in full blown tears. I remember thinking that it is not OK for a cheerleader to be showing sadness, but I couldn't control it. This was the end of four, very dedicated years with the Luvabulls. I had attended practices sometimes until one in the morning, taught in our junior program, made hundreds of appearances, traveled half-way around the world to perform at international basketball tournaments, and all the while I kept a full-time job. There was much hugging between my teammates and me and no need for words.

Five years earlier, in 1998, I was a rookie professional cheerleader in the NBA with the Milwaukee Bucks Energee! dance team. That year my goal was to train and learn whatever I needed to in order to make the Chicago Luvabulls the next season. The Chicago Bulls were led by Michael Jordan, arguably the most famous basketball player in the world. Jordan had led the Bulls to six championships. Chicago offered the best celebrity status and most opportunity at the time for a professional cheerleader. My dream was to be in Chicago and be a part of the Luvabulls. Not only did I make that dream come true, but I was named captain after my rookie year.

I spent a total of five years as an NBA cheerleader with a body in peak physical condition. I could jump off a chair into the splits and had a stomach that looked six-pack perfect in a half-top. I graced the cover of a magazine, posters, and websites and performed at elite venues. I was a good dancer and an even better performer. Fans often told me they could spot me from the nosebleed seats because my energy level reached the roof.

As I was retiring in April 2003 from dancing, I was simultaneously signing a contract with the Chicago Blackhawks of the National Hockey League (NHL) and the Chicago Rush of the Arena Football League (AFL) to manage their cheerleading squads. By June of 2003, I had formed Wynning Teams and asked several of my current teammates to join my cheerleading squads. I was realizing the second part to my dancing dream—to be the owner of my own company and train cheerleaders the way I thought it should be done.

An Enlightened Cheerleader

What I wasn't prepared for was becoming the outsider. For the past five years I was completely identified by my body's appearance and performance capabilities. All of the personal attention on me was gone, and the focus had shifted to others in the uniform. By the time I held my first team photo shoot as a director in the fall of 2003, not only had I gained a few pounds, but I was in so much pain I walked on pillows in the morning to lessen the discomfort of getting out of bed. The pain was totally unexpected. Once I stopped training the muscles every day that I needed for dancing, the aches and pains started to break through and reveal the damage I had done by dancing through injuries. My body was no longer masking the pain and compensating the imbalances because I was not using those muscles anymore. I limped around at my day job and then watched from the sidelines as my friends were still dancing. By the third year as director, I had become pregnant, stopped leading the dance practices, and gained 50 pounds. My assistant and good friend, Gloria, took over as choreographer while she was still dancing and looking physically fantastic.

Looking back on these times, I realize that two things were happening: I was discovering there was more to life than our physical bodies, and I resented others for being identified by their bodies and beauty because I didn't have mine anymore. I was in both emotional and physical pain much of the time, suffering over my lost beauty and jealous of how the team bonded together while I remained the outsider looking in. I wasn't special anymore.

Now ten years after the day I stepped off the basketball court and started my company, I rest in a place of joyful contentment about *not being special* even though our society is obsessed with *being special*. Today I am the sum of my youthful focus on outer physical attractiveness and pseudo-celebrity status and my yearning to provide meaning in my life and the lives of others. Depending on the day you ask me about professional cheerleading and other industries that rely heavily on outer appearance, I am against them and for them at the same time. I am truly the sum of my contradictions and yet comfortable with that because it gives me the opportunity to discover who I am and what I stand for. Over the past few years, I have confronted the earlier versions of myself, learned from her, watched her grow, and now understand how I can relate to many different thoughts and feelings all at once.

A most recent and vivid moment for me was during the 2013 Stanley Cup Championship parade in Chicago. I was atop a double-decker bus watching an estimated 2 million people cheer for the Chicago Blackhawks hockey players and their support staff, including the Ice Crew, our group of skating cheerleaders. I stood behind two rookies as they waved to the crowds and soaked up their "15 minutes of fame." When the busses stopped in a private location to drop us off at the rally in Grant Park, the two cheerleaders turned to each other and said, "I want more! I want more!" I was able to be happy for them to experience the rush of the crowd and accolades. I was also able to accept my personal fear of how this will affect their need to have more of the superficial validation. I personally have experienced the "coming down from the high" and the confusion of it when you are unable to process the loss of being special in the uniform. Frequently, I watch other females hit an emotional high because of so much attention while in the uniform, only to crash after they retire or find that the uniform isn't the answer to all their life problems.

Mary Pipher in her book *Writing to Change the World* wrote, "You have something to say that no one else can say." So what can I say that no one else can say? I can tell you about my journey to find true S-P-I-R-I-T as a professional cheerleader, dancer, and entertainment manager. I continue today as a business owner, manager, trainer, pageant director, and expo producer in an industry that depends on a woman's external appearance to make her a "complete package." I have learned why I sometimes resent and champion beautiful women all in the same day. The professional cheerleading industry offers a unique set of circumstances framed inside a short but intense length of time in a woman's life. It cuts to the very core of the biological female—the ability to instantly attract male counterparts based on outer attraction techniques that for thousands of years have provided us with the ability to reproduce and be physically protected. It is basic instinct, yet it produces very sophisticated systems, ideas, and emotions in our society, where today, we don't necessarily need a man for reproduction and protection.

I have been blessed with being on both sides of the proverbial "fishbowl" as both the professional cheerleader and the director who observes and leads others through the same experience. About five years into being a director, I became a *Philosophical Cheerleader*. First I studied psychology-based disciplines like emotional intelligence, team-building, and how females relate to each other. This research originally helped me to begin to understand female behavior in groups and possibly solutions to conflict and self-esteem issues. Still I felt like there was a question I wasn't asking, something that was missing in my research. The question became, why am I even doing this? What is my deeper purpose for being with all these women during this unique time in their lives?

I started to look for deeper answers, answers that could only be found at the spiritual level. I sought out and studied the wisdom that has survived through the ages. I asked questions and started looking for deeper meaning in my life experiences and the experiences of the women I was training. I experienced a spiritual awareness, deeper than just a philosophical point of view that resonated with the core of my being. This core of my being was dormant up to this point in my life, and it was so freeing to the point that I had to write about it. I feel now that I am working daily on becoming an *Enlightened Cheerleader* and that professional cheerleading can offer an amazing experience that encapsulates more than just the perfecting of one's outward appearance. I began to share with my teams what I now deem as *The Invisible Cheerleader* and my formula for living at the upper edge of our potential ability.

After years of soul searching, I realize that the Universe doesn't care what we do or how we do it, just that we express truthfully to ourselves and others whatever it is that we are experiencing. Shedding light on your personal truth liberates you and gives you a freedom that, literally, no man can take away. By exposing my personal development and discoveries, I hope to serve my gender. All females can discover and reveal their deeper side while simultaneously reaching the peak of their physical confidence. Beauty and brains are not mutually exclusive. The focus on one to the exclusion of the other is always detrimental to our personal development.

The purpose of this book is to share my experiences and bring insight to females about their inner self that connects us to each other and ultimately to the space between the stars. Many of us are mostly unconscious of our inner self because so much of the focus is on our outer shell development and our Egos. This book combines my private, personal search for my inner soul, and the unique way I discovered it while in the outwardly focused professional cheerleading and sports world. This contradiction has been the ultimate teacher for me to find my way. I would not change a moment of my life in the professional cheer/dance industry because by embracing both the dark and light sides of this experience, I have found enough awareness about myself to say something to you that only I can say.

2

ONCE A CHEERLEADER, ALWAYS A CHEERLEADER

In my fifteen-plus years in the pro-cheerleading industry, I have repeatedly asked myself, why do I do this? Why do they (other females) do this? Why does popular society still support, in fact, have a high regard for, pro-cheerleading? Today's young women have every opportunity to leave the sidelines and be an active participant on the field or court. The gender barrier has been broken wide open, and we see women compete in all forms of professional sports, from tennis to golf to hockey. So, why do some women chose to "stay on the sidelines"? I think there are several reasons, but first it seems necessary to tell a bit of history about this industry.

Ironically, the first group of cheerleaders was an all-male group. This first creative group of cheerleading men originated at the University of Minnesota. Their purpose was to lead the crowd in support of their team. Many years ago, young women, who were most likely frustrated

Wynne Marie Lacey

by a lack of women's sports, found an opportunity to express themselves by joining in with the males and doing the cheer leading, tumbling, and gymnastics.

Just like other female sports, such as hockey, cheerleading has a long history that has evolved from a male-created model. Unlike all other sports, professional cheerleading is no longer a male sport; in fact, many argue that cheerleading isn't a sport at all. There are men who are cheerleaders, but never an all-male group. Male cheerleaders are on squads to add power and assist females and the females remain the focus. Today's youngest of females are moving into competitive cheerleading squads that don't actually support a team sport of any kind. They literally just cheer to compete amongst themselves. The current wave of youth cheerleaders is doing it for the teamwork and athletic development. They might never end up on the sidelines.

The professional level cheerleader is every bit as athletic as the next female professional athlete. However, today's professional cheerleaders are less known for their athletic abilities and more for being exhibitionists of physical beauty. This was caused by the National Football League (NFL) which began organizing professional cheer teams in the 1960s. In the 1970s, the Dallas Cowboys Cheerleaders (DCC) emerged with revealing outfits and were seen by the nation at SuperBowl X. This caused the image of cheerleaders to permanently change, and many other NFL teams began emulating the DCC's attire and routines. The DCC cheerleaders resemble today's professional dance teams much more than the earlier Minnesota cheerleaders, whose moves and chants were designed solely to encourage crowd support during team play.

Many professional sports dancers cringe when they hear the word "cheerleader" to describe their craft, but truthfully, most fans label us as "cheerleaders" because that is the origin of the professional sports team entertainer. The NBA cheerleading squads are more specific about

An Enlightened Cheerleader

labeling themselves officially as dancers, but I guarantee every NBA dancer has had a fan ask them on more than one occasion if they are "one of the (insert your team)'s cheerleaders." Many professional cheerleaders will dance for both an NFL and NBA team over their career because very often the type of dancing is the same, and the dancer will want to experience both opportunities.

Cheerleaders are professionals; I have no doubt about that. I know first-hand the work and dedication that goes into the craft of being a professional cheerleader. This work happens at night and on the weekends because most of the women are working another job or going to college during the day. The skills learned while a professional cheerleader are many and easily transferrable to other careers. But, professional cheerleading is not meant to be a career itself, just a unique part-time job that can help in a female's future endeavors. And, I don't think it's the skills we acquire that draw young women to professional cheerleading. I believe that it is the venue that attracts most women to this industry. There are a variety of venues in which to dance and entertain, but there is something about sports arenas. Sports are everywhere. There is a whole section of the newspaper devoted to sports. Athletes are celebrities. The people in our lives talk about their favorite teams that they have loyally followed since their parents took them to their first game. Sports have crowds with amazing energy and bring all sorts of people together in one place for one reason, and it creates an immediate sense of community.

More importantly, professional cheerleading offers a local celebrity appeal that doesn't happen in other venues. Every professional cheerleader is highlighted by their sports organization. The women are put on websites to draw in more hits. They are put on posters and calendars for sponsorship deals. Thousands of these posters and calendars are printed for the cheerleaders to sign at appearances throughout the season. This

9

doesn't happen at dance classes, cheerleading competitions, or the park district recreation leagues.

I think what also draws most women to the professional level today is that they see their particular sport, whether it be dancing, cheering, or ice skating, as an opportunity to do what they loved doing in their childhood. In a recent response to a 2013 RedEye blogger's comments about suggesting that the NHL's Chicago Blackhawks ambassadors, the Ice Crew, should be dismissed, one fan responded with his experience coaching an Ice Crew member. Before being on the Ice Crew, this particular team member (Yanina) had previously been a hockey player on local club team. The coach wrote, "I coached Yanina a few times, and she is a phenomenal hockey player. The media ignores women's professional sports leagues almost entirely, so the Ice Crew is probably the closest chance a female hockey player can get to skating on a professional ice surface." (RedEye blog April 2013)

After years of women's equal rights movements, some people have expressed to me that professional cheerleaders are the living dinosaurs of American sports. I hear genuine concern that in the midst of our growing awareness about the unfairness and destructiveness of traditional definitions of masculinity and femininity, cheerleaders stand out as symbols of the past by serving as attractive showpieces for the teams they represent. That is an opinion I hear at least a few times a year from fans as I walk through the halls of the United Center during Chicago Blackhawks games. But 99% of the time cheerleaders are praised for their ability to add to the fan's experience. Professional cheerleaders are ambassadors for the organization they represent. They are the "front porch" to the house, the first point of contact for the fans. As players move quickly on and off the field, enter their cars from secure entrances, and go home, the cheerleaders are the ones greeting fans or making eye contact while performing from the sidelines.

An Enlightened Cheerleader

The experience of being a professional cheerleader is one I will never forget. Since retiring in 2003, I haven't had any similar experiences remotely like the ones I had in my life when I wore the uniform. It is an inside joke among many retired professional cheerleaders that "once a cheerleader, always a cheerleader." One former NFL Atlanta Falcons cheerleader, Michele "Mickey" Crawford-Carnegie decided to start an alumni membership group (www.alumnicheerleaders.com), offering continued support of our shared experience.

Crawford coined her experience of transitioning from seven years in the NFL to retirement as "After the Poms." Crawford says, "Just like it is difficult for many athletes to transition after playing, the same can be true for us too after we retire." Who better to "cheer" each other up than a former cheerleader? Through newsletters and alumni reunions, this membership group supports and spotlights retirees that are still living their lives in the same high-energy manner as when they were active professionals. One of my favorite pieces from the site is called "Motivational Mondays." It is written by Tina Pulley, a former Kansas City Chiefs Cheerleader and fellow life coach.

Alumni Cheerleaders highlights the many alumni who have gone on to make a difference in the world, specifically because of the skills they took away from the job. One example is Darlene Cavalier, a former NBA Philadelphia 76ers professional cheerleader, who created the Science Cheerleaders. This group is made up of current or retired professional cheerleaders who serve to get the science policy conversation going, solicit views from all sides, and change the tone of science and science policy in this country. They hold a Big Cheer for Science every year that kicks-off the USA Science and Engineering Festival where thousands of kids learn the Big Cheer! They also do many appearances at schools and sporting events to bring attention to many different fields of science.

Wynne Marie Lacey

Cavalier is a great example of how to use professional cheerleading skills to share her passion and get people excited about science. She saw a need to unite the citizens' desire to be heard and valued, the scientists' growing interest in the public's involvement, and the government's need to garner public support for the sciences. To help make this happen, she uses her academic aptitude acquired at the University of Pennsylvania, the mass reach of Disney where she works, and the in-your-face, pom-pom waving personality of a 76ers cheerleader to kick-start the process.

For those alumni cheerleaders who don't make their own waves like Cavalier, many end up in industries that actively seek them out to help sell their product. I personally have known many professional cheerleaders who were recruited into the medical sales market because of their attention getting skills and polished mannerisms. Industry professionals, who have asked me for referrals, say they seek out cheerleaders because of their intellect but even more so because of the emotional connection that cheerleaders can make with other people. The main purpose of any professional cheerleader is to make the face-to-face connection with the fans since the players are usually not accessible. This ability to make fans feel special can translate nicely into a job later on that requires face-to-face contact to get a product sold.

My previous reasons for being drawn to the professional cheerleading world in 1998 will be laid out in the next couple chapters. But today in 2013, I am drawn to the spiritual side of working with groups of young women in high energy environments. I have seen over and over how women can come together and do amazing things when combining their positive energy. I view this energy as a larger *Spirit, or Inspiration,* that is present in all living things. Once spirit is gathered it can move freely between physical systems in order to do its work. You can't see it, but when you have access to it, it gives you passion, and the desire to do the right thing.

An Enlightened Cheerleader

At summer cheerleading and dance camps I attended in my youth, there was always a prize called the Spirit Stick given to the team with the best overall attitude. Supposedly, the Spirit Stick was created back in 1954 at a National Cheerleading Association (NCA) Cheer camp, where one team stood out among the rest—not because of their talent, but rather for their positive and energetic attitude. They were the backbone of the camp; they were always first to arrive to the morning classes, last to leave, and always cheering for other teams. Even though they were not very physically skilled, they were able to symbolize the "spirit" of cheerleaders. They couldn't be recognized with scores or trophies, so the director Lawrence "Herkie" Herkimer reached for a twig off a tree, declared it a Spirit Stick, and awarded it to the team. Since then, the NCA Spirit Stick has become a red, white, and blue wooden dowel and an integral part of the summer camp honors.

We cheerleaders recognize that spirit, positive gathered energy, makes a difference. Why else would we be at a sports event screaming, encouraging, and purposely directing our own energies onto our teams? If we didn't believe we made a difference, we would just sit there quietly and observe. Spirit produces an attitude of, "Yes I/We can, and I/We will enjoy doing it. So can you. And if you do it better than me/us, I/We still win. I/We love being alive and experiencing all that this moment is."

This gathered energy is what I call working with the *Invisible Cheerleader*. The *Invisible Cheerleader* is energy in pure potential form and available to all of us. It is waiting to be used at any moment. When you align yourself with this energy, it starts working for you in ways you never imagined were possible. Adopting a new attitude towards this invisible friend allows you to become a more enlightened person. You will no longer feel sometimes that you are losing and will also realize that in the end, winning is an illusion.

Wynne Marie Lacey

Using the *Invisible Cheerleader* has helped me evolve into a more enlightened cheerleader. An enlightened cheerleader is an oxymoron, because when enlightened you do not conform to a group identity or identify with a label such as "cheerleader." Within these pages I talk about how contradictory I am, and how the sum of my contradictions is what makes me able to share a wisdom I had not encountered before. After reaching this point of new understanding, I now have a deep yearning to share my new found wisdom. At first I knew that all people should be included in what I knew, but then I experienced sadness because this new understanding that is available to everyone is experienced by only a few. This sadness turned into joy and purposeful action by pointing the way for me to write this book.

I don't know if you can ever reach pure *Enlightenment*. But there is a point in which you move to a level of awareness in which you cannot go back, and the rest of your life becomes a search to live more enlightened than the day before. This more enlightened lifestyle means that you have a personal confidence that cannot be shaken by the external ups and downs of life. You know with absolute certainty that you are more than your physical body, and that Spirit lives within each of us. There is a quest to engage in purposeful, present moments, to love yourself unconditionally, and finally, to transcend suffering of any kind. You know you are totally responsible for yourself, and because of an invisible connection we all share, you are bound to improve the whole of society through your own efforts of self-development. Because we are connected, when you choose more right conduct, I benefit. As I chose more right conduct, you benefit.

Knowing what right conduct is for you will become much more apparent when you allow yourself to be guided by the *Invisible Cheerleader* that resides in you and all around you. Even when you accept that *you are a soul that has a body instead of a body that has a*

14

soul, the magic of the Universe is still a mystery. But you are content with not knowing *how* it works but knowing *that* it works! It is a point of self-illumination in which you know who you are exactly and are totally OK with not knowing the what, where, when, how, or why. And since once a cheerleader, always a cheerleader, my excitement about this can't be contained. I want to shout it from the rooftops and spread the good news!

Self-illumination can happen when a person is faced with repeated situations that feel internally wrong for them, but there is no logical reason for it to be so. Stories of self-illumination are usually about men wandering alone in deserts for 40 years, leading thousands from bondage, climbing mountains solo, hearing from burning bushes, or leaving majestic palaces to sit under a tree and ponder the wonders of the Universe. These journeys are very individualistic, private, and inwardly-focused. My journey towards enlightenment is very private as well. But many of my own self-illuminating moments occurred within a fifty mile radius of my house. Sometimes self-illumination occurred when I was surrounded by over 22,000 screaming fans in the United Center. I learned I could experience lonely feelings around thousands of people. It was these very non-logical moments that helped me discover, unravel, and reveal that which was true for me.

As a professional cheerleader and director, I have been involved in very disconnected situations in which I felt like a fraud, fake, or untrue to my inner-self. A professional cheerleader, by definition, is a brand concept. They are the human expression of what a sports organization values and promotes. The cheerleader is not asked what her values are or what she stands for; in fact, it's better if she doesn't express her personal feelings at all. This was actually the perfect storm for me. Because I am always asking questions, it was the ideal place for me to ask why I felt so awkward internally while loving the outward attention I got in the

Wynne Marie Lacey

uniform. I began to notice over the years as a director, that there were common challenges that all cheerleaders (and other people who choose situations where they are judged on their appearance like models and pageant participants) were subjected to:

1) Losing her personal identity because team unity and outer expression demand that she is more aligned with the brand concept than her inner values. Often we identify ourselves by what we do, which causes a condition of being a specified person without permission to be different than what is defined for us by the group. Ironically, we can only define ourselves when we are in relation to other people. This book will offer solutions on how to be in pursuit of what you as an individual identify with but not to make it your entire identity.

2) Losing contact with her personal values because she is told/taught/expected to foster another's agenda before her own, even though it may be in conflict with her own agenda. This book will offer solutions to become involved with, but detached from, other's values so as not to mistake them for your own. Young people these days don't have a singular moral authority like religion. They are being directed to be their own personal authority. Because young people hang out with young people, they pick up values that are not tried, true, and tested and sometimes are distorted by social media. This book offers a wiser perspective than may be found on your friend's Facebook page.

3) Having too much emphasis on the outer shell and physical presentation and less importance placed on inner development. This book offers solutions on how to experience the value of seeing yourself as a soul that has a body, not a body that has a soul. Your soul can and should be the lead in your life. Your body

An Enlightened Cheerleader

and its physical appearance can be compared to an envelope that can take you half-way around the world. But when that package arrives, it is what's inside that anyone really cares about.

4) Experiencing unnatural competitive situations between teammates and team to team. Success that requires another female's failure is usually uncomfortable to our gender's natural state. We need to remember that winning the spot on the team or the Miss America crown is the result of a judge's subjective opinion. This book offers solutions on how to cooperate and get closer to your goals instead of competing with the women in your personal life, workplace, and social settings.

5) Having only one expression to work with—being happy, and the sadness that comes with not being able to sustain it. This book shows you what happiness really is, how your pursuit of happiness is a pattern, and why welcoming unhappy moments is a part of what makes you human and drives you to the next happy experience.

The struggles of the professional cheerleading industry offered the very conditions that I personally needed to find the *Invisible Cheerleader*. So much emphasis on the visible always made me question the energy I sensed in people but couldn't see. I knew spirit was there, moving in and out of me and others. I knew we exchanged energy because it manifested visibly and moved through crowds in the form of cheers and chants that moved players to do their best. This sent me on a journey to want to know for myself what breathed life into me and made me whole. It now gives me the desire to explain to others how to get the *Invisible Cheerleader* to work positively in their lives. I have felt it work in my life and bring about sweeping changes that keep me searching for a deeper connection. It is my sincere desire to help you reach this same level of peace and joy.

3

IF YOU ARE HAPPY AND YOU KNOW IT—SAVOR IT

Cheerleaders are the happiest outwardly appearing athletes in the sports world. They are not afforded the expression of a range of emotions. It's just happy all the time, and that's it. My mother told me once that it is futile to try to be happy all the time. Happiness is a fleeting state. One should strive, instead, to be content within oneself. Content means to be quietly satisfied. Cheerleaders are almost never quiet or content, and certainly rarely satisfied. I thought up until a few years ago that my mom just didn't get it, and her view of happiness was just plain sad. I am writing this now with the personal discovery that my mom, of course, was right.

Our Declaration of Independence states that we have these certain inalienable rights—Life, Liberty and the Pursuit of Happiness. At first glance there is that word—Happiness! But really "the pursuit of" happiness is one of our inalienable rights. Pursuit means the chase, the hunt, the search for, the tracking down of and detection of something. That is what we are endowed with by our Divine Designer—the act of chasing our dreams, our desires and moments of happiness. There is no guarantee you will actually find it (or bottle it and sell it for that matter).

Michael J. Fox, who is publically dealing with Parkinson's disease stated recently in an interview with *AARP Magazine,* "my happiness grows in direct proportion to my acceptance and in inverse proportion to my expectations. That's the key for me. If I can accept the truth of 'this is what I'm facing – not what can I expect but what I am experiencing now' – then I have all the freedom to do other things." What Fox is saying is that we have the freedom to pursue our happiness but freedom means different things to different people. When you can define freedom for yourself, not what is written in the constitution or a dictionary, your happiness might grow, too.

The Buddhist tradition indicates that the pursuit of happiness is *desire*, and it is desire which causes our suffering. In a collection of Alan Watts lectures, Watts speaks to this:

"Now this is the Buddhist trick: the Buddha said, 'We suffer because we desire. If you can give up desire, you won't suffer.' But he didn't say that as the last word; he said that as the opening step of a dialogue. Because if you say that to someone, they're going to come back after a while and say 'Yes, but now I'm desiring not to desire.' And so the Buddha will answer, 'Well at last you're beginning to understand the point.' Because you can't give up desire. Why would you try to do that? It's already desire."

This statement by the Buddha explains how there is contradiction in the pursuit of happiness. We desire to be happy, but this can only lead us to first discover what makes us unhappy. It is a cycle that is not

An Enlightened Cheerleader

meant to be broken. We are built to desire, get what we want, feel a new desire, get what we want, and continue until we die. The part that society forgets to tell us is that we must have unhappiness to get happy; the two are totally connected. We must first experience the unpleasant, uncomfortable feeling of being unhappy or unfulfilled because this is the precise tool our body uses to get us to change our behavior and take a new action that serves us better.

For example, I remember when I desired to audition for the Luvabulls. I wasn't aware of being happy or sad per se, but when I heard that I was cut at one point during the audition process, I became unhappy. This unhappy feeling drove me to audition for the Milwaukee Bucks. At first, I was happy on their team. Then I became unhappy because it was a long drive from Chicago to Milwaukee, and I really just wanted to be a Luvabull. I became unhappy enough that I auditioned again for the Luvabulls and made it! That made me really happy! Then the experience on the Luvabulls was harder than I thought it would be, and that made me unhappy. This unhappiness drove me to start my own company and become a Director so I could lead women in a way that I thought promoted self-respect and a loving attitude.

The Buddha doesn't want you to let go of your desire for happiness. But I think the Buddha does want us to see the cycle for what it is. The Buddhist proverb continues with, "Pain is inevitable, suffering is optional." Johnathan Lockwood Huie explains: "Pain is what the world inflicts upon us. Suffering is our emotional reaction when we fail to make the difficult conscious decision to choose Joy". Suffering, moving away from happiness, happens in one of two ways: Either you are *not* controlling your own emotional reactions, *or* you are trying to control that which you are not in control of (which is everyone and everything else). Suffering is optional. Happiness is optional. Joy is also an option. Start to see that these are your choices.

21

Wynne Marie Lacey

I have followed my own trail of breadcrumbs to go backward and discover those turning points that have made me both happy and unhappy. Becoming aware of these turning points and using this new awareness as I move forward has brought about a beautiful, wonderful state of contentment. Contentment is the destination. The verb action I like to take to achieve contentment is *savor*. Savor means to relish, delight, treasure, cherish, and appreciate when you are able to produce a happy thought, feeling or special moment. In *Buddha's Brain*, Rick Hanson speaks to the power of savoring. Hanson calls it "internalizing the positive". He says instead of suppressing negative experiences (which is not really possible because what you resist will persist), foster positive experiences, and "take them in so they become a permanent part of you."

One way to savor life is to slow down and just take the time to notice that positive experiences are all around us. This happens naturally for most of us as we get older. I remember as a young person driving a car, I would sometimes get stuck behind an elderly person and wanted to say to them, "Your life is almost over! You should be driving as fast as you can! Don't be going slow and wasting time!" I was always in such a hurry, packing in as much as possible in each day until I passed out from exhaustion at night. Now I think it is very possible that those elders were savoring that moment, happy that they were still driving at their age and for their personal freedom. If you don't take time to savor moments like this in life, you will feel you are missing out, you are unsatisfied with your life, and you will continue to suffer.

On the other hand, reaching for happiness every single moment of my life has caused me much suffering. When my agenda was to create nothing but happiness, I didn't acknowledge that unhappiness is just as important a part of life to experience. Much of the time I would look around and see only that which caused me sadness and would think— it's time to fix it. Being happy to me meant overcoming a sad state and

An Enlightened Cheerleader

replacing what was making me sad with something that would make me happy. I couldn't stand being unhappy. It was uncomfortable, and I wanted it gone. I could replace a person, place, or thing and get a temporary state of happiness. But nothing lasts forever. I started to see that being happiness is a temporary state.

I started to think being unhappy could actually be welcomed and expected. It is healthy to experience unhappiness because it means you are capable of understanding what makes you happy. When at a point of not knowing what you want, let that feeling challenge you to change direction and attitude. It can lead you to the state of contentment my mother was always speaking about. I realize that to experience happy moments I most certainly needed to expect and, in fact, welcome feelings of unhappiness. That is the only way for us to discern what happiness feels, looks, smells, sounds, and tastes like.

I found an inner peace knowing that happiness and unhappiness are just on opposite sides of the *same* spectrum. When things are on the same spectrum that means they are related to and highly connected to each other. There can't be one without the other. I am certain you could easily recall a person who originally you felt very happy around but at another time felt the extreme opposite. The person, place, or thing can be the same, but we have decidedly fluctuated along the spectrum of happiness.

One of the exercises I would challenge you to do is to follow your trail of breadcrumbs backward. Find each uptick in your life. Was there a particular theme to how you achieved happy moments? How did your brain categorize what you were experiencing in those moments? It might just show you the sum of who you are up to this point in your life.

The theme of my life's pursuit of happiness can be generally summed up by the terms *leadership* and *external validation*. I have been from one end to the other of the happiness/unhappiness spectrum while in leadership positions. While developing the foundations of

Wynne Marie Lacey

my Ego (which means how one defines the self apart from others) as a child and young adult, I was thrust into leadership positions that made me feel all kinds of happiness. As I got older I allowed myself to believe the programming that leading others must be what made me happiest. When I was the leader, I took charge of my own happiness. I found more control in my level of happiness if I was in charge of all the situations I was involved in. Once I became in charge of myself and others, I felt very confident I could make others happy with my decision making abilities.

I was the youngest child in my family, so my first taste of leadership came in fifth grade as head of the coveted Ice Cream Sales position. Once a week, I got out of class early to unlock the freezer, load up the carts, and head to the lunch room to sell goodies for 10¢ apiece. I got to pick two classmates to assist me each time. Everyone was happy to get ice cream. The teachers were happy to see me take my responsibility seriously. The kids I picked to help me each week were happy to get out of class early. Happy was the theme of this position. There was no opposite that I can recall.

As I moved into junior high school, I became a leader on the volleyball team. I think I instinctively understood that if all six of us worked together on the court we would do better than if we had individualized goals. I would get the girls into a huddle and put our hands together. Standing in that circle with hands on one another's was one of my first moments of understanding that we are more than just our physical bodies. We were energy in motion (e-motion), and I could feel their energies on the court. When our energies were aligned, we would do our best, and more often than not, would win the game. I could feel that we were going to win before we actually won the game. There wasn't a rational, logical reason or statistics that would tell me this; it was a certain feeling in the air.

An Enlightened Cheerleader

In high school I became the captain of the dance/pom-pom squad. I loved this position and dedicated myself to this team and placed its importance way above my academics (Sorry, Mom). We went to the state competition for the first time and started a tradition in our school that still continues to this day. If there were unhappy times, I do not remember them for the happiness is what is lodged in my memory banks.

My next leadership position came as pledge president of my sorority in college. By the time of reaching adulthood, I was certain I had leadership as a strength. We had a great time that year, winning a coveted spot in the National Multiple Sclerosis Charity Drive event to compete live on MTV's Spring Break Lip Service Show televised nationally. In every case of leadership up to this point, I had somehow inspired others and helped to create many moments of happiness for myself and others. I don't remember ever promoting myself or trying to understand why people looked at me as a leader or why others felt comfortable having me in a power-wielding position.

All that changed when I experienced my next leadership position. I spent three years on an NBA dance team as a captain. Here I discovered that my leadership style clashed with that of the director and her choreographer. This made me very unhappy. In fact, I probably had as many unhappy moments as I had happy moments. And when I had unhappy moments, I usually shared it with the rest of the team. I viewed the director as leading with fear-based tactics instead of the happy, loving energy I had used in all my previous leadership positions. Up to this point in my life, I had led myself and others with a loving approach and with a love for the act we were doing. I didn't fully comprehend my leadership style until I experienced being unhappy. What had given me happy moments all my life wasn't the leadership but the *way* I led others.

25

Wynne Marie Lacey

When I lead with love and my natural state of being, I am happy. When I lead with fear and force, I am unhappy.

Leading myself and others with fear was a new experience for me. I saw it on one hand to be effective, initially providing better and faster results. When new women came on the team, they would lose weight, become better dancers and better performers. We were scared to death to mess up; we knew we could easily be replaced. The director encouraged me to rattle the rookies and be hard on teammates to keep producing results. In fact, one season the director championed a veteran who prided herself on dancing for weeks with walking pneumonia because it showed her dedication.

The problem was that myself and many others on the team felt unhappy. Many of us would console each other outside of practice through long bouts of crying and complaining. Our boyfriends would ask us repeatedly why we put up with the perceived emotional abuse. Towards the end of my last year, our unhappiness spilled out uncontrollably in mean email campaigns and a secret meeting with our director's boss. Nothing changed, and we just continued to spiral into unhappy rants.

Somehow we figured that laughing at our director's expense and performing in spite of her would make us happier. It didn't. Spite isn't a happiness factor for me. But I continued to use it because I saw it as one of my perceived limited options. One day I ended up walking out of practice. I sat on a set of stairs outside the room for quite some time deliberating whether to quit or go back in and "take it." I went back to practice and pouted for attention and soon was pulled out for having a bad attitude. I decided to speak up for myself and my teammates and air our grievances. I was given a very stern talking to about how our team's demand for respectful treatment titled us "spoiled brats." For the

26

An Enlightened Cheerleader

rest of the season I had to stand in the back of the room during practice with the rookies for my disloyal act.

I didn't quit. I stayed and had an amazing twist of events while I finished the season. Our director also worked with another team of professional sports cheerleaders in the Arena Football League (AFL). The AFL staff approached me to take over the contract for the next season. Here came my perfect opportunity to go back to leading with love instead of fear. I started my company Wynning Teams in 2003, which I still run today. I have worked with hundreds of women and five major sports teams. When I first set out to start as a director of a dance team, many of my friends came along with me from another dance team because I had convinced them that we, as a team, were going to make a better situation for ourselves. We were going to have a fun and positive environment with better instruction and overall attitude. It worked because I fully expressed my vulnerability, lack of experience, and my need to make them satisfied. I attempted to be the facilitator, not the dictator.

As the years went by, I had to step back from the group and take away my intimate friendships, and I was viewed much more harshly. Even though I had the same goals and wanted the best for the women, my vision to them became distorted when they saw me as something different. I was becoming the nagger about weight, being on-time, understanding their responsibilities to the sports franchise, and the one who judged them.

As our team got more competitive to make and the games produced alternates, I had to separate myself from them. Not having peer to peer relations with the young women became important so as not to be seen as favoring one over the other. But this lack of emotional connection and me being all business had the team losing respect for me. I had become what I viewed my prior director as being. I understood now why the previous director had used many of the tactics she had. I am sure after years of dealing with the same situations as I was encountering, it is easier for her to shut herself off to the women than to open herself up for more and more personal hurt.

Many times team members feel victimized and bond during the stressful times in a negative way—through bitchfests over the leader or leaders they feel powerless against. Women only want women leaders to use their power as a way to increase resources equally. Women are not comfortable when a female leader uses more masculine approaches. If women see you as a directing and controlling leader, most will see you as the proverbial "bitch."

My intent as the leader back then was to make every female that came under my leadership better for it, and at the very least, happy and loved. In reality, there are many more cases than I would like to admit when happy outcomes didn't happen. My personal suffering came from trying to control what was not in my control—the happiness of others. At the same time, I wasn't concentrating on what made me happy, which is the only thing I can control.

Around 2008, I started becoming very unhappy in my Wynning Teams' quest for Total Domination of Happiness. Something was definitely not right. I started researching emotional intelligence and the dynamics of teams, especially female teams. I became a certified Life Coach and starting preaching sermons about how emotionally inept we females are. More and more I was unable to relate to or make the women on my teams happy. I was so concerned with being the *one*; the one who made life better, easier, and more fun for these women. The more I tried, the worse it got. So I then turned inward and concentrated on making myself happy.

But I wasn't happy all the time and faking it really sucked. And that is how I started thinking that maybe my mom had a point; it isn't

An Enlightened Cheerleader

realistic to always be happy, and we should strive to feel content. But professional cheerleaders and dancers don't lead with content. They lead with loud bursts of energy, smiles, sharing good feelings with fans, and all the right moves. Unhappy is not an acceptable part of the job description. Where was the happy medium for me? I felt my purpose was to bring unconditional support and love to others, but mostly I was telling women to shove those unhappy moments under the rug and put on the happy face for fans.

I began to feel alone in the professional sports world. Those lonely moments brought on thoughts that I better get out of this business because I couldn't relate to it anymore. I had moments of seeing professional sports and their entertainers as being some distorted and absurd illusion. I couldn't agree with what I was doing anymore and how I was portraying women in society. Then the next day I would be so proud of an email I received from a happy client that stated how the cheerleaders had made an impact at a charity event. I would see pictures and be dazzled by the beauty caught by a photographer who posted their pictures. Sometimes a cheerleader would confide in me about her personal life. When I had deep conversations with team members about struggles they were having outside of the job, I would feel a sense of purpose.

The best moments I experienced were watching dancers on the football field when they rocked a routine. As Phil Jackson wrote about professional basketball players in *Eleven Rings*, "What moves me is watching young men bond together and tap into the magic that arises when they focus—with their whole heart and soul—on something greater than themselves. Once you've experienced that, it's something you never forget." That same "magic" that Jackson is referring to is present with cheerleaders and dancers, too. And I agree it is something I have never forgotten. It is a big reason why I want to further the

Wynne Marie Lacey

sports performer whether she is a dancer, ice skater, cheerleader, or promotional member.

I started to accept that to really make an impact, I had to be in contact with, be an influence on, and actually stay in this business to do it. In my experience, we are contradictory by nature and nurture. And it is something to know about yourself so you can define your personal truth. The professional cheerleading and sports world is a breeding ground to see what is and is not your personal truth.

Today, I have found a happy medium, a sense of contentment within myself at the tender age of forty-two. The power of contentment, of enlightening oneself, does not have to occur in a monastery somewhere or on a spiritual retreat. It can occur slowly, every day with awareness, humility and the pursuit of happiness. I have stayed in the professional cheerleading world because as the Zen saying goes, "Before enlightenment, chop wood, carry water. After enlightenment, chop wood, carry water." Staying where I am and on task to spread the light is how I find my purpose in the world and show others how to do the very same thing. The Universe wants us to find moments of happiness in all walks of life. It doesn't care where we do it—only that we do it. This just happens to be where I am today. Where I am tomorrow is an experience I am looking forward to having and not being in control of whether it is in the cheerleading industry or somewhere else. That is the gift of enlightenment—being OK no matter where you are. If you just show up and be interested in who or what is in front of you, wondrous things can happen!

4

THE TOTAL PACKAGE IS ONLY THE ENVELOPE

The public image of professional cheerleaders is only seen as "happy." Rarely can a professional cheerleader portray her unhappiness or a personal opinion. While the players on the team are allowed to show their pursuit of happiness, their disappointment when they don't attain a win, their personal opinions, their imperfections, their likes and dislikes, the cheerleader remains steadfast in her same outward expression—happy.

A professional sports organization brands the female ambassador through the use of the uniform, making her the "front porch", so to speak, to their million-dollar investment. Being the front porch of an organization puts the cheerleader in a sometimes confusing position without understanding how it is affecting them subconsciously. Before becoming a professional cheerleader, a female is usually promoting the "self" through her own desires, growth, and development. When one

31

Wynne Marie Lacey

becomes a professional cheerleader, she must fit into someone else's version of who they want her to present to the public eye.

This is "concept promotion" versus "self-promotion," and many cheerleaders find this confusing to the point of losing their personal sense of identity and sometimes their individual self-worth they obtained before making the professional team. As young females move into adulthood they may not be able to fully accept themselves. Therefore, they can distort a spot on a professional team as making them whole or more acceptable to society. When ladies make a team, they usually experience a sense of euphoria and feel very special. I often see this early euphoria downward spiral into, "I am still not good enough," when comparing themselves to the beautiful and talented women they now call their teammates. Cheerleaders by definition are uncritical, enthusiastic supporters of others and their goals, and for some reason they have the hardest time giving themselves that same unconditional love and support.

When I am hired to train someone who wants to audition for a professional team or if I hold a prep class for my own upcoming auditions, we cover the same four principles each time: 1) Hair and makeup presentation, 2) body fitness and awareness, 3) talent and 4) overall presentation of the physical self in a feminine manner. They are based on physical appeal and outward projection because that is what is judged during an actual pro-cheerleading audition.

If at auditions the judges subjectively find the candidate to be successful in these four areas, we move to the interview process and look for signs of mental and emotional healthy self-esteem. But if she is someone who unconditionally loves her total "self," she actually may not be right for this job. A professional cheerleader must always be willing and responsive to follow other people's view of how to present her "self." For example, we'd have no Justin Beiber or Timberlake if those boys

An Enlightened Cheerleader

were content to sing alone in the shower. The validation of their fans is most likely the driving force behind why they share their talents on such a broad scale and tolerate all the invasion of their privacy. Because outer validation is such a huge driver in society, it is probably the main reason why they started their careers so young.

Hair and makeup on a cheerleader must be her tools to add a sense of glamour to herself. Professional cheerleaders are supposed to immediately grab attention as they walk into a room. When representing a professional male sports team whose main purpose is to win, the female counterparts must "win" the male's attention. Adding a sense of glamour, by definition, gives that irresistible alluring quality that somebody possesses by virtue of seeming much more exciting, romantic, or fashionable than ordinary people. Cheerleaders can't be ordinary; they must seem special.

One of my current team members is absolutely stunning with no makeup on and freshly combed hair. I can admire her, but I know that it isn't "professional" for her to be in her uniform without putting on at least a little makeup and teasing her hair. Fans will think she doesn't care about impressing them if she doesn't try to doll herself up. The guys on the team are giving it all they've got to win, so she should be doing all she can to win her game. This sort of attitude makes me cringe when I think of it, and it is ironic that it is one of my own attitudes!

When I made a professional team at the age of 27, I had never really worn makeup. I remember standing in a line during an audition finals and having the director walk up to me, grimace, and ask if I was willing to pluck my eyebrows and wear eyebrow pencil. Of course, I said, anything to make this team. It wasn't at that exact moment that I felt I was a less beautiful member of the female species without makeup, it was after repeatedly wearing lots of makeup that I felt that way. When I wasn't wearing the makeup, I felt less than pretty because I now felt

Wynne Marie Lacey

I needed to wear makeup to be seen by fans and be acceptable. I still have a hard time walking out the door without at least some mascara and lip liner on.

The cheerleader's body shape is mostly based on society's view found in advertisements and TV shows. It is a combination of muscular tone and a flat stomach. She must also be comfortable wearing a minimum amount of clothing and standing upright and confident. No holding her arms across her stomach because she feels awkward. You can't feel awkward in front of 20,000 fans or be pulling at your uniform to hide a muffin top.

Depending on the requirement, audition candidates are expected to show their dance or skating skills at a certain level of mastery. And the dancing and skating should be done in a feminine manner. At ice skating auditions, I will see an amazing female hockey skater on the ice wearing a simple t-shirt. Simultaneously I will see a less skilled recreational skater with bling on her sports bra. Judges will always prefer the more feminine person. At dance auditions, I might encounter an amazing freestyle break-dancer in baggy clothes and a less skilled, skinny blonde who has the potential to do a double turn if I work with her a lot at practice. Again, I am more likely to select the soft glamour of the skinny blonde.

When the team is announced, I feel sad for those who are not chosen. I am concerned that those who are turned away view those that are selected as the "better" end of the female spectrum. I personally don't want any woman leaving an audition feeling they are less than another woman. There is a certain level of distortion in professional cheerleading, as in all groups of athletes or performers, because they are heavily judged on one area of success. I can see this, but I resent it. I also recognize the sports industry supports a one-sided view of males as being heroic when competitive and brutal. Together the combination puts

An Enlightened Cheerleader

females on one side of the spectrum by being cooperative, supportive, submissive and eye-pleasing to men. At the same time they are on the fringe of the male spectrum that champions competition and physical domination.

During the audition process, we usually send out announcements stating we are searching for those females that are the "Total Package." Sometimes I feel like changing the wording in the audition announcement to "Walking Billboard" or "Eye Candy." What I want to advertise to young, impressionable females is that the "total package" is really only the envelope that encases the important document. It is external. The envelope will take you far, half-way around the world if you want and back. But in the end, the envelope falls away, is throw in the garbage, and all anybody really cares about is what the envelope is carrying.

This envelope is necessary to carry you and should be cared for. Being exceptionally attractive is one temporary way to be successful. There is no doubt that female beauty is real and wonderful. My husband jokes that I am more interested in looking at females than men. And it is true. Women are beautiful, and I love to look at them. But I also love looking at birds and great art and rainbows. Getting a spot on a professional cheerleader squad is one way of receiving outside validation that you are attractive to the male species. It is not the only way and in some ways not that important. But it is a level of success in one piece to the female puzzle.

More important to this point is that it is just one piece to the puzzle of a life and just one place to be for a short time in a life. It is not forever. It is to be experienced and celebrated but not made someone's total personal identity. This isn't the only type of success to experience, nor should this be called the best years of someone's life. In a professional cheerleading job, the female is occupying her shell of appearance. If

35

Wynne Marie Lacey

at the same time the cheerleader is not building the internal parts of who she is, she will trap herself in her shell. It is just as important to learn how smart she can be, what challenges her mentally, what interests can be conquered, what her personal boundaries are, what mountains there are to climb, and what valleys she can endure. These goals help find someone's personal truth. This also helps the cheerleader to be emotionally healthy and able to leave the profession, or any other appearance-driven situation, gracefully.

Focusing on my particular experience, I now see it for what it was. It was, first and foremost, me reaching the pinnacle of my potential outward presentation. It depended largely on outside validation from others in our society, especially from a certain group of males. It was finding success in building the shell but not the person.

My industry only promotes a part of the female. In the past, I have loved being glamorous and being asked for my autograph. In recent years, I have worried that I am portraying women to the public as sex objects and second class citizens to professional athletes. I shared my inner conflict with a very open-minded friend. She suggested that before I quit working in this industry, I needed to unconditionally love these women whom I managed and trained. I had to love their quirks, the way they worried about their bloated stomachs and pimples on their forehead that no one else noticed. I had to love them when they went back to their abusive boyfriends, got promotions to senior managers at work, took another bartending job, won reality TV shows, and also when they graduated from law school. They are diverse and they are complicated and they are just trying to figure it out the best they can with what they know to be true. When I stopped judging them and what I do, I felt it was right for me personally to spend my precious time here on earth with professional cheerleaders.

An Enlightened Cheerleader

As I started to truly love these women with the unconditional love that I feel for my daughter, I began to love spending time around them. I loved hearing about all their challenges and loved seeing them have happy moments as professional cheerleaders. Being around for their unhappy moments gave me the opportunity to help bring clarity and compassion to their situation. My desire to help people gain balance in their lives and seeing how wonderful each person is individually became my reason for staying in the industry.

I began to see that a woman can learn about her inner self while being a professional cheerleader. Cheerleaders develop the ability to entertain audiences and attract attention with physical expression. But they also develop personality traits that encourage relationship building and becoming aware of others in relation to themselves. Here are some of the traits that I have discovered cheerleaders around the world share:

The Ability to Relate/Connect to People: One of the ladies on my team remarked that she is able to "have a conversation with a soda can." At her young age she can strike up a conversation with anybody, anywhere. In the age of technology where most communication is one-sided and not face-to-face, this is a real skill. Most of the time we are not interacting with the people in our physical proximity directly. We are more likely to be emailing or texting someone far away on the other end of their laptop or cellphone.

The Ability to be a Team Player: Within the microcosm of the team, we learn that we are only as good as the sum of our parts. Our rewards are based on collective performance, and we can accomplish more together than we can alone. Phil Jackson, famous NBA coach, said it is "…essential for athletes to learn to open their hearts so that they can collaborate with one another

Wynne Marie Lacey

in a meaningful way." Jackson goes on to relay that when a teammate is working to their highest potential, not only does he or she transcend their own limitations but helps bring up the potential of each member of the rest of the team. I have seen this time and again as a dancer myself and also on my dance teams through their physical abilities. Those members who learn to reach their full inner potentials find it will spill over into the rest of their lives and their relationships.

The Ability to Control Our Emotions: Because the job description of a cheerleader only allows for one expression, happiness, we have a lot more control over our thoughts and emotions than we think we do. Many times, all around the world, a cheerleader walks into the locker room to change into her uniform drowning in a bad mood. By the time she leaves the locker room, she is smiling from ear to ear. Though this is a temporary fix, it teaches us that in any moment, we can change and control our energy. This is a sort of virtue, an admirable quality. "Virtue simply involves regulating your actions, words, and thoughts to create benefits rather than harms for yourself and others" (Hanson 2009).

The Ability to Practice Self-Discipline: We are pleasing to watch, and we entertain. That comes with practice and dedication to someone else's teachings. We can practice self-discipline at all times in order to search our inner selves and find our unique expression. Over time one can develop an emotional, mental, and spiritual connection and then express it to others. Self-discipline can come in handy when we search for meaning and purpose. We can be a great ambassador for others, but we can also use that talent to see what we can develop and express in our unique selves.

The Ability to Hold and Foster Another's Agenda: The sports team's mission is not our personal agenda. We don't create it or own it, but we do have the power to care for it. We add a high energy. We love our teams no matter if we win or lose. We are unconditionally supportive. Holding someone else's agenda with detached involvement is a wonderful way to be supportive of someone's decisions and choices without making them your own. We can also communicate for those who can't. Cheerleaders are the direct connection from the team to the fans. The fans who come into a building to watch a game are much more likely to come in contact with the cheerleaders than with the staff or players. You can translate this type of "face time" to something you are passionate about. It is very likely you will become the person in front getting others to pay attention. Like Cavalier and the Science Cheerleaders, we can all use our "pom-pom waving" style to bring attention to something we care about in a way that only we can.

The Ability to Define what is Right for Me: While I was being directed to fit into the cheerleader's mold and be similar to those around me, I was able to observe what felt right for me on the inside. I was able to see my personal boundaries, and I saw others find their personal boundaries, too. I remember one year our LuvaBulls choreographer had put together a dance that used the American Flag as a prop. At one point, the flag dropped to the ground, and we drug it along the floor. One dancer pointed out that this was disrespectful to do to our flag and felt veterans in the audience would be offended. When the choreographer wouldn't change the choreography, the dancer pulled herself from the routine and took a stand. She just couldn't bring herself to disrespect the flag. The rest of us did the routine. But for her, I think she found a bit of courage that day. As a choreographer and director myself, I have seen other women step up to say that something didn't feel right for them. I have had dancers pull themselves from dances because of feeling a certain move was too personally uncomfortable for them to perform. I have had cheerleaders at promotional appearances in bars call to tell me they were leaving early because they just couldn't take any more of the inebriated and disrespectful patron behavior. An Oklahoma City Thunder Girl cheerleader named Kelsey Williams was recently publically targeted by a female sports blogger for being "too chunky" to be an NBA cheerleader. Blogger Claire Crawford actually asked readers to participate in a poll to see if they felt the cheerleader was either too chunky or the perfect size. Williams commented on her Twitter site, "To be womanly always, discouraged never." Williams was able to define this trial as a way to count her blessings because she received lots of positive feedback for her handling of the situation.

These defining personal moments are done by observing your thoughts and feelings and being authentic in that moment. Yes, you might disappoint somebody and may even lose your job. But at least you will have been true to yourself. In our Divine Design, this is why we are here. I have become more authentic in myself and see the total package of who I am today. I feel whole, consistent, complete, and undivided. I can pass through life with moments of happiness and unhappiness and feel a sense of deep peace along the way. After all the experiences I have had and the rollercoaster of emotions I have felt, I can find that spot of firm ground to stand upon as I move through each incoming

An Enlightened Cheerleader

event. Now no one else has to define for me what to think, feel, or do. Integrity is deeply personal. Only you can define for yourself the path to take, and it doesn't happen overnight. It is to be practiced, cared for, and paid close attention to.

Now I see my time here on earth, whether it be on a dance or cheer team or elsewhere, as an enlightening experience not a defining experience. Any experience I have in relation to others brings about personal discovery opportunities for me. I consciously decide to have these experiences without letting them define or label me. Every experience illuminates my inner self and all the potential that lies within me.

In almost every experience I ask, "How do I want to be in relation to others? What do I value when in relation to others? Do I want to be pretty? healthy? unique? smart? wise? encouraging? competitive? cooperative? spiritual? religious? feminine? Why do I want these things? How does it make me feel inside? What do I value in myself?" I take the experience, add awareness to it, and find a bit of integrity to keep building my inner knowing.

5

THE LIFE FORMULA

There is an ongoing debate, which you have probably heard at least one time in your life, about whether your human behavior is based on genetic predispositions and animal instincts, or if you act the way you do because you were influenced by environmental factors (e.g., caregivers, societal norms, etc.). This debate is called the Nature v. Nurture Theory and neither side has officially won, as of yet. Obviously, we get a lot of our physical characteristics from nature, but where do we get our intelligence, talents, personality traits, and ultimately our desire to know who we are and why we are here? This debate searches for answers so that ultimately, we will know what controls us, and in turn, we will have more control in creating the life we so desire.

I study the Nature v. Nurture question from a different point of view—I don't believe we are the *creators* of our life at all, rather we are the *reactors* to life's unlimited array of experiences. This viewpoint

43

Wynne Marie Lacey

takes some objectivity. Think back in time to the subjective religions and how they used to place us at the center of the Universe. Christian religions taught that the sun revolved around the Earth. When Galileo offered a public, objective, and scientific explanation that suggested the sun was the center of our solar system, this collided with the religious beliefs that humans held the special place in the Universe. This was so contrary to the beliefs of the time that, according to Wikipedia's article on the Galileo Affair, Pope Urban VIII forced Galileo to recant his findings, condemned him from the Catholic Church, and put him on house arrest for declaring that we aren't the center of God's Universe.

We know now that we are the third planet from the sun and one of many solar systems that are contained within the Universe. This knowledge helps us move forward in so many ways, but it originally hurt a lot of people's pride who believed we were the most special thing that existed. So I understand that people might be hurt when I say that you don't really get to create your life from scratch, you just get to react to it.

I think this is a really positive way of looking at life. It allows you more freedom in the way you live each day. If we concentrate less on controlling life and more on how we REACT to life, welcoming all kinds of experiences becomes more fun. All you really need to know is how to be in control of yourself. Why? Because "I" am the only thing I am in control of in any circumstance. That is it. That leaves us 100% in control of our consciousness. Consciousness is our awareness or the perception of what is passing before us at any given moment, and it gives us the ability to have an experience and integrate it into ourselves. Each experience I have makes me unique because I experience it differently from someone else in the same room at the same time. What I am conscious of in a room might be totally different than someone sitting next to me. I might be checking out people's faces in the room, and the person next to me might be checking out the artwork and colors.

An Enlightened Cheerleader

Since my consciousness is the only thing I am in control of at any given moment, doesn't it make sense to really get to know how I perceive life and find out who I really am? How well do you know yourself? If you don't know yourself that well, how can you possibly manage yourself? If you can't manage yourself, then how will you ever bring the best *you* to any given circumstance? You can't *be yourself* if you don't know who you are.

Knowing yourself is to know the greater organizing intelligence that gives life to us and all things. The same intelligence that brought you into this world is the same intelligence that created Earth, my dog, and the trees in my yard. When you are in awe of this invisible intelligence, you can be in awe of yourself because you are it. There is order, patterns, cycles, and purpose to *the you* that is both your limited physical body and your unlimited, larger, conscious awareness. When you acknowledge this, you can become aware of your being, like an observer watching from an objective distance. After you become aware of yourself in a more objective manner, you can start to manage yourself and finally become your own master.

Self-mastery is the ability to get along in a world that is constantly changing and knowing that you can handle yourself in a myriad of situations. You don't deny your feelings of inadequacy built up from your childhood experiences; you simply set out to prove them wrong on a daily basis. You can build up a strong internal resilience even in the wake of feeling vulnerable. I like to think of this process as working towards becoming a *Master Reactor*. I define a Master Reactor as:

A person who has mastered the art of reacting positively to stimulus and change, can behave authentically and consistently no matter what the current influences, and is living at the upper edge of their personal and potential capabilities.

45

Wynne Marie Lacey

In the wake of tragedies like Hurricane Katrina and 9/11, it doesn't always seem like our planet is part of a loving, well-oiled, and highly functioning system—but we truly are. Most people would say it is just the opposite: Every person for themselves! You gotta watch your back and lock your doors, or you will be the victim of somebody somewhere! The world is a random, competitive place and you better get to the finish line first!

I don't believe the natural world is random at all, it just seems that way because we have a limited understanding of the way it works. We definitely take the time to understand our man-made laws in our communities, states, and country because they give some of us a sense of control. But very often we skip over really trying to understand the way natural laws actually rule the planet and our solar system. Man-made laws are weak, many times unbalanced, and just plain unfair, in order to tip the scales towards one group. Man-made laws are subject to interpretation, can't ever solve 100% of any problem, and are always subject to change. Natural laws don't change. Nature is always working towards balance and harmony. You don't have to vote for, abide by, or even believe in natural laws. You are subjected to them whether you like it or not. The key is once you understand the order of the Universe, it becomes that much easier to be a part of it. And it's actually not rocket science.

Some examples of our highly functional and intelligent universe are easily missed if you don't look for them. Nature and universal laws aren't debated within a House of Representatives, aren't lobbied for, and definitely not advertised in the form of billboards or a pop-up ad on the *yahoo!* home page. These laws don't show up on a government website and are definitely not told to you by the police officer who pulls you over to remind you to go the man-made speed limit.

An Enlightened Cheerleader

The Universe runs on *Absolute Truth*. The sun doesn't shine because you believe in it or we made it a law—it just *is*. You and your body are subject to the laws of the sun and other universal factors no matter whether you know it or not. Get to know these absolute truths. You can use this information to help you flow through life instead of always wondering why most things seem out of your control, and why it seems like some people were put on earth just to frustrate you.

The Law of Gravity is a great example of a Universal Law. Gravity is invisible to the naked eye, and we don't feel it with our five senses. This is a law that we didn't create, and we can't destroy it. Nobody wrote it in the Constitution as one of our rights as human beings. No governmental authority had to say that gravity would treat us all equally. But we can all agree that we are very thankful that it exists; even if we wish certain people would fly off the earth now and then.

You don't have to understand how it works. You don't actually have to believe in it. You could deny it on the corner of a busy street with signs that say, "Gravity is a hoax!" or march on Washington D.C. asking for gravity to be banned in the USA. But guess what? You don't get one iota of say about gravity, and that is a good thing! You can't mess with it and screw it up for everybody else. It was, it is, and it always shall be until the *Invisible Cheerleader, or your Higher Power,* decides that it just isn't working for the good of the Universe anymore.

Natural laws are in place for a reason—to assist humans on their journeys. We can't leap tall buildings in a single bound or fly in the air like a bird. Gravity is a powerful law that keeps your body from spinning off into space, and it is to be respected. Being grateful for gravity and its purpose can help you understand why certain laws are set and boundaries are needed. Knowing these natural boundaries gives you the potential to stretch your imagination as far as humanly possible, master your capabilities, and find your life's purpose.

Wynne Marie Lacey

When you think back to being born, you are not conscious of asking for this to happen, right? You are born. Now what do you do? You have these parents you didn't consciously choose. Now what do you believe to be true about your identity? You have these friends who say X, Y, and Z. Now how do you think for yourself? You have these teachers who tell you to learn A, B, and C. What do you do with this information? It is all about how you react to being plopped down in the middle of the Universe.

Here is my simple formula for being conscious of my reactions to daily life:

INTENTION + ENERGY + MATTER
= All Life Expressed on Earth

First, what are the Intentions behind my actions? What are the thoughts I am thinking in my head or saying out loud to others that are motivating my current behavior? For example, when I am asked to watch my neighbor's kids for the tenth time in a row, do I say yes because I love the kids and enjoy having them in my house? Or do I resentfully say yes because I want to be liked by the mom, or because I fear her disapproval of me, or that she will tell the other neighbors I am a bitch and then I will have no friends?

Second, what emotions or Energy does this bring up in me? E-motion is Energy in Motion. When intentions start swirling in my brain, it brings up an e-motion that directs me to take action. What kind of energy and emotions are flowing through me? Am I in control of how I respond? Do I have a choice to pick a different kind of energy or response to my neighbor's request? When I start feeling the fear that nobody will like me if I don't do whatever they ask, do I have to believe it? Can I pick a different emotion to have? Ultimately, can I seek

48

a higher energy like the *Invisible Cheerleader* to help me through the decision-making process?

Third, what are these intentions, thoughts, emotions and feelings doing to my body or Matter? How is my body and brain matter processing this? Is my stomach turning when I think of saying no to my neighbor? Are my palms starting to get sweaty? What can I do to make sure I am listening to my body and helping it calm down through the irrational thoughts? What part of my body is responding? Is there some DNA that makes me want to be a doormat to other people's needs? Is there a part of me that is just been programmed by my parents to be of service to anyone who asks?

When I slow down, even if it's for a deep breath or counting to ten, I get a clearer picture of what my body is processing. These moments when I calm down and take a step back allow me to be more in the present moment. When I am present in the moment, I am more self-aware. The first step to self-mastery is awareness of the self in the present moment. This formula is simple. I will admit though, it is a tough decision to slow down on a daily basis and really get to know yourself and your default tendencies. But I promise, once you start, you will be so happy that you did it.

When we as humans add DISCIPLINE to the equation, we can become Master Reactors and live at the upper edge of our potential capabilities. This formula then becomes:

**DISCIPLINE + Intention + Energy + Matter
= A Master Reactor**

How do I know that you will be happy? Through years of research, life coaching certifications, and personal soul-searching, I have gotten to really know myself and be comfortable in my own skin. It doesn't mean I know everything about myself. I haven't lived my whole life yet, nor have I peeled away every layer. But no one can know me and my experience of the world better than me. And the better I know who I am, the better I am able to share my authentic self and my unique gifts with the world. No one else can do that but me. Everybody else's life has been spoken for. Think about that. No one else can be (state your name here). So what are you waiting for? Did someone tell you not to be you? It is a possibility; most likely someone during your lifetime has innocently or purposely been telling you not to be you.

So let's be our own persons, our own personal cheerleaders, and react to life with the same uncritical, enthusiastic support that cheerleaders give their teams. You didn't consciously choose to be born, to have your parents, or your childhood experiences. Let's start taking back our power and learn how to take control of our reactions to life; so we can thrive, not just survive. Cheerleaders never give up on their teams nor control the outcome of the game, but they just enjoy being a part of it. So enjoy your life whether you consider it a winning or losing game.

6

INTENTIONS: OUT WITH THE OLD, IN WITH THE NEW

Life is set up for you to succeed in whichever way you choose. So what are you choosing? Are you conscious of your intentions; I mean really conscious of what deeply motives you? It is important to be conscious of the intentions behind why you express certain energies and make certain choices. Dr. Wayne Dyer reveals in his book *The Power of Intention* that energy is focused by Intention. That means that the all-powerful *Invisible Cheerleader* is focused by your Intentions. The *Invisible Cheerleader* is non-judgmental, therefore, it doesn't pick which of your intentions are good or bad for you or Earth; it follows your Intentions to the exact measure you put them out into the Universe. Remember the first formula:

INTENTION + ENERGY + MATTER
= All Life Expresses on Earth

Dyer says, "Everything in the universe has intention built into it," and, "This is true for all life forms, whether it be a wildebeest, a rosebush, or a mountain." He goes on to say how a "...tiny acorn with no apparent power to think or make plans for its future contains intention from the invisible field. If you cut the acorn open, you won't see a giant oak tree, but you know it's there." Secondly, Dr. Dyer explains that intention doesn't make mistakes. "The acorn never turns into a pumpkin," and that "every aspect of nature, without exception, has intention built into it, and as far as we can tell, nothing in nature questions its path of intent."

Unlike humans, the acorn that Dr. Dyer refers to doesn't have a consciousness that yearns to be the pumpkin. The acorn doesn't say, "Hey, the grass is greener in the pumpkin patch, and I wish I was over there!" Nor does the acorn desire to be a bigger oak tree than its buddy next to him. This is where our human ego-consciousness is a double-edge sword. Our ego-consciousness gives us the ability to do amazing things, but it also causes us to listen to others' views of ourselves and to worry about the past and the future. Because we can remember the past and see what others have that may seem better right now, we mistakenly yearn for things that may not be right for us in the present moment. When we believe what we have isn't as good as what others have, we can cause ourselves to suffer or think we are less than good enough. We become dis-harmonized with ourselves, even become ill-at-ease when it physically manifests in our body systems.

Today I have an awareness of the unconscious intentions that I carried through high school poms, my college dance team, and finally to the NBA. I personally did not develop a healthy view of myself growing up. My emotional needs were unmet by my busy, working parents, especially my father. During high school especially, my parents had a strained relationship before their divorce, and it wore on our

An Enlightened Cheerleader

family unity. All of us kids were basically searching outside the home for comfort and emotional connection.

In the summer of my freshman year in high school, I developed breasts and received lots of attention from my male friends based on my new sexuality. There was a very real outward validation from the boys that my fellow female friends were not receiving at the same time, and I began to see how important my feminine features were. These moments began replacing that less desirable view I had of myself at home. I found that I did like male approval, and more importantly, I was fearful of male disapproval.

When I was growing up, my older brother was the primary and most important male role model in my life. I sought his approval daily from the moment I could walk and follow him around the house as a toddler. I was constantly trying to please him. I would prepare and serve him his food and drinks, sometimes do his chores, and play whatever games he wanted to play. As we got older, I did what he thought would make me popular in school and made sure I was friends with his friends. I wouldn't defy my brother's view of who he wanted me to be. In fact, without ever being interested in dancing as a child, I tried out for the school dance team because he suggested it would make me popular.

When he went off to college, I was no longer under his constant guidance, and I turned towards other males my age to find my worth and validation. I fell into believing that I needed to please a boyfriend and lost my virginity to him. When my brother came home from college that summer, he found out through our common friends that I was no longer a virgin. I vividly remember standing on the porch outside my backdoor and seeing my brother's face as he told me I had "ruined" myself. Even though at the same age he had openly admitted to losing his virginity and "became a man," I, however, had ruined myself. Since my brother was the one I sought approval from, you can imagine that

Wynne Marie Lacey

this crushed me. It also built some resentment in me because he didn't view himself the same way. Why could he lose his virginity, and it be a good thing? And when I lost my virginity, it was a bad thing?

He didn't talk to me for 3 days (which was an eternity), and our relationship felt strained after that. All judgment of myself regarding this issue was tied up intricately with my brother, and I had disappointed him. It has taken me a long time to see how, from that point on, I programmed myself around male approval, wanted to serve males, and also resented that they were the gender able to express their sexuality freely. I have since become aware of my default tendencies towards men in general. As a professional cheerleader, I wanted a man to desire me for my appearance but then got mad if they dismissed the mental and emotional parts of me. These contradictions piled up, and the more they did, the more complicated I made my personal life.

Truthfully, in the end, I wanted to experience both types of validation in my life. I wanted to be attractive to men because of my physical appearance, and I wanted to be attractive to men because of what came out of my mouth or how I interacted with them in other environments. Sometimes those things happened separately, sometimes at the same time, but many times not at all. Now I am aware that my intentions were caused by my insecurities; I see that I can have a new intention around building my self-worth. I now intend to think differently and acknowledge that I am worth more to the Universe than what a passing man thinks of my body. The past intentions don't control me now or cause lasting disappointment when I am not the center of male attention.

The first step I took was to become aware of my intentions. I had to understand where they came from, how they developed, and finally not be ashamed to admit that they were different than what I was projecting to the outside world. Once I did that for myself, it gave me

An Enlightened Cheerleader

an amazing sense of control. No longer did I have to act in a way that was uncomfortable to me or behave in a way that labeled me. I was free to choose whatever way I wanted to move forward, even if it was totally different than what others expected from me.

OLD INTENTION: Seek outside validation from all males who I allow to put themselves in positions of power over me. Use my feminine charms to get what I want and to feel special.

NEW INTENTION: Allow myself to let go of the past and move forward with the intention of building my own self-worth that can then be expressed through healthy relationships with males, especially focusing on my husband, son, father, brother, and friends.

Some women are uncomfortable with their sexuality and find it easier to express it though the "cheerleader mask" because we are growing up in a post-feminist world. Many women have been programmed as young girls to work harder on their brains and physical skills while ignoring the benefits of an attractive appearance. It's as if beautiful women get things because they are beautiful and lucky, and smart women get things because they accomplish it themselves through hard work.

One professional cheerleader who was finishing law school explained to me that she was, in fact, uncomfortable with her sexuality and needed an outlet to feel free to express her beauty. In law school and in the courtroom, she didn't feel able to be the total of who she was. She felt she could only be smart and confident. In her job as a professional cheerleader, she found that she could express her feminine, less domineering side. Because our society subtly tells females that we cannot be both, we believe it. She commented that she heard more disrespectful comments from fellow lawyers in the courtroom about her natural beauty than from inebriated bar patrons while at appearances

55

Wynne Marie Lacey

as a professional cheerleader. She seemed to be expressing to me that it was almost disrespectful to be beautiful in the courtroom because it distracted others. She heard about this over and over from fellow lawyers.

This particular cheerleader had been changing her expression of herself to make men feel comfortable in her presence, whether at the bar or in the courtroom. She toned down her beauty in the courtroom to avoid attention and toned down her intellectual conversations in the bar. This was her choice, and that is something to take note of—we have the freedom as women to be as expressive as we want to be. It is only ourselves who are holding us back from being all that we want to be in any situation.

OLD INTENTION: Tone down her beauty in the courtroom and tone down her intelligence in the uniform to make others feel comfortable and accept her in either situation.

POSSIBLE NEW INTENTION: Bring all of herself to every situation in a way that doesn't threaten her self-worth and shows the world that female confidence can be inspiring and benefit others.

I have also come across many cheerleaders who have very strained relationships with their mothers and now find it hard to trust the actions of other females in their life. They never felt safe around the unconditional love of a mother. These women on my teams are often the ones who become overly competitive with other teammates because they never experienced the warmth of their mothers' care, nurturing, and support. Unconscious, protective intentions develop based on feeling frightened, not being able to experience unconditional love, being vulnerable, and rejected.

An Enlightened Cheerleader

Over time I have watched professional cheerleaders, estranged from their mothers, be more difficult to get along with. These women show a real desire to "do it themselves" and less desire to fit in with the team. A general distrust of females occurs with these women, and they often feel more comfortable around men. This can cause many different scenarios. These women relate to men better than women, so they are seen as catering to men and putting themselves and men above the tight-knit group of teammates.

OLD INTENTION: Do it all herself because other women cannot be trusted with her most intimate feelings and vulnerabilities. She must protect herself.

POSSIBLE NEW INTENTION: Be open to developing trusting relationships with both females and males that will allow her to be who she feels she is emotionally, to make mistakes, and to find a safe place of non-judgment.

We all have the ability to uncover the unconscious motivations in ourselves. When you acknowledge and bring them to light, they stop controlling you. Motivations that I encourage you to let go of are the ones that produce extrinsic, temporary prizes like money, good grades, power, or status for a brief time. Extrinsic motivators are temporary and cannot take the place of doing an activity that we find rewarding internally. Start identifying those tasks in your life that will be rewarding to you if you did them in a dark cave all by yourself. When experiences are internally rewarding, no one can take them away from you.

Alfie Kohn says, "Escaping this trap ultimately means finding more successful ways of securing our self-esteem; building an unconditional sense of trust in ourselves that will make it unnecessary to keep demonstrating our superiority." Instead of waiting for others to accept

Wynne Marie Lacey

us, we can accept and love ourselves, and only then can we accept others, as well.

The steps to accepting ourselves aren't always easy to take, but they are worth it! It is not a one-time validation and then you are set for life, either. But we have to start somewhere, sometime; I encourage you to start right now. The *Invisible Cheerleader* wants nothing more than for you to validate yourself because that validates the work done by the Creator itself! It will be up to you to define your relationship with the *Invisible Cheerleader* and how it works in your life. When you find a joy, a desire that no one or thing or event can take away from you, you have found the connection to your *Higher Self* where intentions can be made in a more positive, supportive, and life-enhancing way.

7

ENERGY: THE EQUAL PLAYING FIELD

I believe everyone's life purpose is to be in harmonious relation with each other and the planet. But this is not to say that life itself is fair, and we are all created equal. Fairness is an illusion. If life were fair, I think our society would look *much* different. I think it would be rather boring. Many times the greatest moments happen specifically because life is not fair, and people succeed despite amazing odds. Examples include the football game where the underdogs are down by 30 and ended up winning, or the minority kid who grew up poor and became our 44th president.

New people and experiences come into our lives to replenish us and so does Energy. Energy is the one source that is fair and equitable to each of us. When we add our Intentions to Energy, it shows *how* we relate to one another and the world around us. Self-relation and relationships with others are governed by Laws of Energy. Energy is

59

Wynne Marie Lacey

invisible, but it directs how you and everything you see appear in the world. Your body is visible matter, just like a rock on the ground. Energy is usually invisible and resides in your intentions, thoughts, and feelings, and it then becomes visible through your actions. Remember the simple formula:

INTENTION + ENERGY + MATTER
= All Life Expressed on Earth

You are the exact expression of the energy you have taken in up to this exact moment you are reading this. E.C. Pielou explains,"Energy plus matter has constituted the whole content of this Universe." Energy gives us and everything on the planet movement.

Take gasoline for an example:

Intention	Matter	Energy	Expression with Purpose
Want to get from A to B as quickly and efficiently as possible	Car	Gasoline	Moving car from A to B

I can have the intention of wanting to drive from A to B. I can have a car to drive from A to B. But if I don't have the gasoline, or energy, I can't get the car to move or get the result I want. Furthermore, to get there efficiently and without breakdown, I have to have the right type of gas for the intended use.

This example explains how your body works, as well. Science uses two types of energy to categorize what is available to us—anabolic and catabolic. Anabolic energy is simply loving, creative, healing thoughts and feelings that expand a piece of matter, namely you. Catabolic energy is destructive, constricting thoughts and feelings that drive the adrenaline hormones in your body to break down the reserves of energy in your body when faced with a physical or emotional threat. Cycling

60

An Enlightened Cheerleader

these energies through the body is a good thing so that we don't end up with a traffic jam of one or the other type. However, when too much catabolic energy stays within the body, Bruce Schneider explains that it starts to "actually cannibalize our entire system."

Anabolic	Catabolic
Love	Fear
Cooperation, Building, Renewing, Healing, Growing	Competition, Fight, Flight, Victim, Break-down

Think of catabolic energy as the defensive front line of a football team—always pushing and forcing to hold their boundary and sack the quarterback. It is exhausting to watch, and they are only concerned with taking out the quarterback and stopping others from achieving their goal of a touchdown. Anabolic energy is more like the quarterback of the offense—dropping back, looking at the big picture and finding any opportunity that opens up for him to pass the ball.

A real life example of energy exchange is how we change a carrot, which has chemical potential energy, into usable energy by consciously chewing it and letting our body unconsciously take over and digest it. We get to choose what we eat, but the body does the work for us. And from there, you can choose how to use the new energy in your body, whether you sit on the couch watching TV all day or run in a marathon. We know individually what gives us the best energy to do our chosen tasks.

The same way we fuel our bodies to do physical work can be applied to our mental and emotional energy. What thought "carrots" and corresponding emotional "carrots" do I feed myself? Catabolic energy can be present in your life without any immediate physical threats. It can come in thought form as limiting beliefs, assumptions, misinterpretations, and philosophies that are not in line with your personal truth. If you have filled up your potential energy with catabolic

Wynne Marie Lacey

thoughts like: Someone else has to lose for me to win, I have to fight for what I want, I am not good enough, and I am too fat, ugly, and stupid. Then guess what? Only that is what is available for you to burn up as energy. If you are receiving frustration in your life, it is because you are accepting or creating frustration.

The output of your thoughts and emotions can only be that which is potentially available in your body in the first place. If you have the thought, "My life sucks and this is stressful," then this is the only output option you have to use. It's the Universal Law of Energy. We know we get to choose our thoughts, right? And you have access to every thought there ever was or ever will be. So choose! Schneider also says, "With choice comes freedom." And now you know that you are 100% responsible for your energy intake and output. To summarize, you are either having life-enhancing thoughts, feelings, and behaviors, *or* life-consuming thoughts, feelings, and behaviors. In the most basic terms, it is your personal truth versus falsehood.

Catabolic thoughts find that everything is false or wrong until proven true. Anabolic thoughts break through that resistance to life. Any internal issues that come up are faced, and we learn from our experiences instead of our judgment of right and wrong. It is constant self-correction to the point of self-mastery. When you are having anabolic thoughts, you know you are responsible for your own happiness, and love is created within and cannot be taken away. Life will be less about forcing and pushing for what you want and more about using your passion.

This energy exchange sounds so easy, doesn't it? So why is it so hard? Energy is subject to *friction*. In science, researchers can apply perfect conditions to energy. A pendulum can be suspended from a perfectly frictionless bearing, and it will swing forever. But E.C. Pielou reminds us that, "in real life, with conditions unavoidably less than perfect,

An Enlightened Cheerleader

this does not happen." In everyday life, energy is subjected to friction, drained away, and must be refilled either by pushing or pulling the pendulum. You know this intimately with your own body because you have to constantly refuel yourself with food and exercise. The same is true for your mental and emotional input and output. You must constantly be thinking positive thoughts to have forward movement. You must become your own master by thinking about whatever serves you best and that you can change what you think whenever you want. Think of your thought choices like a buffet in front of you at all times. It is your choice what you put on your plate and when to say, "No thanks."

Our mental friction also comes in the form of emotional responses. Thoughts stir up excitement, sadness, love, fear, and a myriad of other forms of energy that either expand you or contract you. And because we are subject to the Universal Law of Friction, we must constantly choose to renew our thoughts and commit to achieving our highest potential. Just like taking a shower to stay clean and healthy, you must constantly renew your positive thoughts and emotional responses. It takes self-awareness followed by self-discipline.

Friction can be the fear in our lives that slows us down, makes us aware of our fragile nature, and stops us from driving our car off a cliff. But it is when we keep our foot on the brake, step on the gas at the same time, and hope to move forward, that we are no longer flowing with our natural laws. We must take our foot off the unhappy brake to move forward. It is certainly necessary and natural to use and experience both types of energy. We are not above nature or the rules of this planet. Nature and its laws do not bend to us. The more we understand our limitations, ironically, the more we can accomplish on earth because we are working with our conditional nature rather than fighting against it.

Working with energy is like having an actual cheerleader standing behind you, always cheering you on, wishing the best for you, and

Wynne Marie Lacey

constantly reminding you to have a positive outlook until the game is over. We don't have that other person with us at all times, but we have constant access to the *Invisible Cheerleader*.

My Definition of ENERGY (i.e., the Invisible Cheerleader):

The *Invisible Cheerleader* defies the limits of a worded definition. Feeling its power and influence in your life is based on individual experiences that words fail to completely communicate. Compare it to the ocean. Since our souls are part of the *Invisible Cheerleader* and can't be separated from it, think of your individual soul as a wave or ripple in the ocean that rises up and then disappears as soon as someone tries to measure or label it.

Your physical body can be thought of as a boat on the ocean, and your Ego (sense of separate self) is the captain of your vessel. We need our Ego in this life to desire the boat to turn one way or another. Your loving soul will either provide calm waters or knock-you-over waves depending on how well you are following your life's purpose. Our soul, with a deep love, prefers you to go with the ocean flow and let its waves of wisdom guide you. However, if you decide that you will defy the ocean and its plan for you, it most certainly will alter your course. This is when we suffer. We fight what is happening to us instead of trying to understand it and its lesson. Beautiful surrender and smooth sailing is a choice as much as defiance and struggle are choices.

It sounds contradictory. But practice surrendering your life to the *Invisible Cheerleader,* and there will be more joy. And this joy is something within you, so it is completely protected from worldly

64

An Enlightened Cheerleader

changes. This perspective can show you that it doesn't matter what you do or where you do it—just *how* you do it. Do you meet life with love or fear?

You stay in the boat on the water with your Ego as captain. But through appreciating the ocean and its dominance, you can enjoy the ride a whole lot more. Every new person and situation you encounter without effort and negativity seems divinely put in your path. You will start to feel like you are watching your life unfold more than having to force things to go one way or another.

If this sounds good to you, I would encourage you to connect more with the *Invisible Cheerleader*. This can be done in many ways. But the first step is to be *aware*. Start seeing what is really true and what is just a perception of your brain or Ego. Anything that needs constant defense is an illusion, simply because it is not real. If you have to defend a belief you have about yourself or others, know that is *not* Truth.

Just for today, anytime you feel the need to defend a thought, feeling, behavior or action, know it isn't your Truth. When you feel less than whole, know it is some false belief you hold that tells you that you are less than whole. It is not the truth of who you really are. *A Course in Miracles* tells us, "You were given everything when you were created, just as everyone was." You only need to restore your awareness to this fact. Once you start this journey, restoring the awareness you had when you were first born, life starts making sense. When life makes sense, you can move forward with a deep, inner confidence and choices become of a higher order.

8

MATTER: THE TEMPORARY BOUNDARY

You are encased in Matter, a temporary, physical boundary which very often we refer to as Me, Myself, or I. Who exactly is the "self?" Who answers *me* when *I* talk to *myself*? Who am *I* talking to exactly? Have you ever said something like, "Ouch! *My* foot is killing *me*!"? If your foot is a part of you, then who is the "Me" that is hurting? When you say, "My foot is killing me," it is an immediate separation of the foot from the rest of your body. "Me" doesn't like the uncomfortable feeling of pain, so in that moment there is a verbal separation between "Me" and my foot. You go to a doctor, plop your foot on the table, and take no responsibility for it anymore. You tell the doctor to fix this foot with a medicine or a surgery. It bothers "Me." I can't cut it off, and I don't want to do what my body might be telling me do (i.e., rest it on the couch for a week). So Doctor, please fix it.

Wynne Marie Lacey

The emotional pains we feel, we will also try to separate from, by first putting that emotion on someone else—blaming them for the way we feel because the "Me" doesn't want to be uncomfortable. But unlike going to the doctor, that other person we put the blame on doesn't fix the problem. So we sit, we stew, we agonize even to the point of suffering because we are unwilling to take on the responsibility ourselves and listen to what our emotions are telling us. We might end up at a psychiatrist's office getting pain or anxiety medication in order to take the pain away. The pain is still there, but we cannot deal with it anymore; it must be compartmentalized and ultimately someone else's responsibility to fix. It is just not acceptable for the "Me" to have these feelings and be OK with them. Why does this happen?

"Me" resides in the brain and compartmentalizes your perception of the world. Your brain classifies, catalogs, labels, and groups experiences in order to better understand the world it is trying to fit your physical body into. "Me" fears, judges, analyzes, wonders what others think, takes things personally, and is housed by the brain. In *Buddha's Brain*, Hanson and Mendius explain that your brain is an amazing piece of complicated machinery that not only regulates itself but all other bodily systems through learning and selection.

Our society puts the brain at the center of our personal universe and consciousness. The brain is very, very important, and you can't live without it. But just because you can't live without it, doesn't mean it should be left to run the body without a checks and balances system. Just as there is a President of the United States who gets to make the final decisions, it is only after much deliberation and agreement between the other branches of government. And just like the president, you have the right to vote another way. Our democratic government takes so long to make adjustments because so many voices are involved in the process. This is a good thing because our history shows that dictators

An Enlightened Cheerleader

and kings are not best for the whole of society. Your brain wants to be the dictator of the total you, but it should be a partner—a tool in the ongoing development that is you.

Jeffrey Schwartz and Rebecca Gladding wrote a book called *You are not Your Brain* which explains how the brain is in charge only because we allow it to be. And "Left to its own devices, your brain can cause you to believe things that are not true." Your brain regulates itself. Your brain doesn't ask your inner being which direction to proceed in at a given moment. Your brain is efficient. It does some amazing stuff without you even being aware of it. Your brain commands the electric pulses that beat your heart, heals your wounds, digests your food, and all the other bodily functions you don't consciously think about. It does its job without asking permission because it can. It doesn't need your approval.

The secret that your brain doesn't want you to know is that your consciousness actually has power over it. Your brain knows this little secret, so it keeps you unconscious most of the time. Think of it as Dr. Brain who gives you a sedative so you don't hurt your body and stay protected. The brain will use fear-based messages to keep you safe because that has worked for thousands of years in our world of real dangers. You better be afraid of the lion that wants to eat you and the stove that is going to burn your hand if you touch it. However, Schwartz and Gladding go on to explain that we end up with a cycle of overly protective and "...deceptive brain messages." They define deceptive brain messages as "...any false or inaccurate thought or any unhelpful or distracting impulse, urge, or desire that takes you away from your true goals and intentions in life (i.e., your true self)."

These constant brain sedatives are actually masking connections to a Higher Self and the *Invisible Cheerleader* that connects us to all things in the Universe. Your soul knows your purpose in life, and it quietly

Wynne Marie Lacey

stands by waiting for you to notice it. Your brain's job is important and bossy. But it has limits just like the rest of your body. By becoming aware of *all* of you, you can become friends with the brain and direct it to be a partner in the process that includes your Higher Self.

The brain is where language is processed and formed, so it uses words all day long to get your attention. But it is not in charge of you and your purpose for being on Earth. Do not, I repeat, *do not* believe your brain's desire to keep you safe through fear. It is not always the best idea. Notice that when you are talking to yourself, there are at least two of you, and you don't *have* to listen to either one of them!

Schwartz and Gladding explain how even when you acknowledge that the brain messages might be false, you can't control or even stop them from coming. Your brain has been in control of you your whole life. "You can't make your thoughts or urges disappear by using willpower alone." You will just add to your frustration by trying and failing to do so. Your control lies in your power to veto, just like the president does. You have a choice as to how you respond to these deceptive brain messages. "Using Veto Power, our minds can influence our actions after the brain generates the initial signals to get our attention."

There are at least two of you—a brain constructed story of yourself called the Ego and what is referred to as the Higher Self that goes beyond the body. Never having actually seen my own brain, I have faith that when scientists say you have a left brain and a right brain, it is biologically true. Many experts put your left brain (LB) in charge of the past and future. LB is the part that analyzes everything that is happening to, around, and in you through your five senses. LB processes, analyzes, compartmentalizes, and prepares for events. LB uses language to get your attention. LB is one of your BFFs. It never stops learning how to fit into society and be more efficient at whatever you set your mind to accomplish. It is there to remind you how to ride

An Enlightened Cheerleader

a bike even if you haven't been on one in a couple of years. LB sees the approaching bike, loads the file to ride the bike, and you ride just like the last time you rode a bike. And if you learn a new trick, it stores the new trick for you to use next time.

LB learns by watching your parents, caregivers, TV, teachers, coaches, friends, and every other person that has ever been in contact with you. The downside? LB is only as good as its environmental influences. LB would be very different had you been switched at birth with the family down the hall having a baby the same day. The upside to being influenced by your environment? You have the power to control LB's intake, which means you are in charge of your environment. You can keep what is expanding and serving you today. Uproot and throw away what is not. Think of it as deleting the junk emails.

The decision to delete or keep some programming is done by the right brain (RB). RB uses feelings to get your attention. RB, similar to the moon, is circling, watching, and pulling the tides of your emotions. Experts say your abstract thinking, creativity, and feelings reside in RB. LB can analyze every logical thought, but until you incorporate your feelings, you have access to only half of your brain's potential. You can sit around all day thinking, but it is the e-motion that moves you to action. You can talk all day to someone about what love is, but until that other person has experienced the feeling of being in love, they will not be able to fully comprehend it. Feelings anchor thoughts in the body and make it real and unique to you.

You can't prove a feeling to anyone. You can't reason with your feelings. You can't write it in a book or post it on a blog and then believe that another person has the same knowledge or understanding of the feeling as you. Feelings are universal, but they occur to people at different times while reacting to different things. It is up to you to decide what makes your body feel happy, sad, angry, and loved. It must

Wynne Marie Lacey

be experienced inside your individual body. You can't scientifically prove to another that you love them. You just know it. And many times you know that you don't love that person anymore. It is just gone. You can't even explain it. It's just the way it is. These feelings in the RB are a key way to bring you into the present moment when most of the time our LB is analyzing the past or the future. Feelings give you a real time indication in the present moment so the whole body knows how it is doing in relation to its environment.

Sometimes we are thinking about the past, and it gives us a current feeling of sadness, frustration, or guilt. Schwartz and Gladding call these false "emotional sensations" that are brought on by deceptive brain messages. This is confusing. You might think you should still be sad when recalling a past experience in which you were feeling sad. But the truth is, the RB is just reminding you that that feeling occurred when you had that experience. It is not necessarily what the body is feeling in the present moment.

In the simplest terms, your brain has expectations and will limit you to experiencing life with less than an open and trusting heart. The brain has expectations based on learned behaviors from previous interactions. It stands alert to protect your body and the very definition of who you are. Hanson and Mendius remind us that the brain sends very real, sometimes uncomfortable, even agonizing alarm signals to pulse through your nervous system to set you back on track. Racing heart, queasy stomach, sweaty palms, and shortness of breath can be the result of deceptive brain messages that are based on protection. These uncomfortable, sometimes very painful feelings, are a form of motivation to get you moving in a different direction. Sometimes it takes a moment to step back and see the feelings that are occurring are a result of your brain's expectations instead of real danger or a need to do something different. Sometimes you can sit through the discomfort

An Enlightened Cheerleader

and teach your brain a new way of dealing with the situation in front of you.

The brain communicates to the rest of your body through your nervous system, and as Hanson and Mendius mention, it "…moves information around like your heart moves blood around." When you have a thought, it travels throughout your body via the nervous system and causes physical responses. So when the "Me" in your head wants to remember a dance or ride a bike, it sends the stored knowledge through a series of signals throughout your nervous system. It also sends signals for everything that it thinks automatically.

Let's take an example of me, a dancer, at practice. The choreographer says we are going to review a particular dance that I had learned previously. As I retrieved it from my memory, an emotional tie of having had a hard time learning the dance popped up, and I immediately tightened up and felt nervous. Now at this moment I could just accept what my brain signals are sending, which is fear. Mostly likely I will make mistakes because in the past I had difficultly learning the dance. But in this present moment I could think a different thought. I can think to myself, "Relax, you got this; we learned this already. I am fully engaged and ready to do this dance the best I have ever done it."

The point here is to see that the brain is giving me what it knows to be true from past experience. It absolutely gives the facts of what it knows. It tells me that I know the dance, but that when I learned it, it was hard for my body to coordinate it. And I feared it. Thanks, brain! Awesome! I appreciate the feedback and the memory! Now I am going to move forward with new thoughts, new ability, and trust in myself to do it better. This time when I do it, I am going to relax first and give myself the opportunity to excel in this dance. When I replace the old, fear-based thought with a new, positively powered thought, it gives me a whole new chance to do it better.

Wynne Marie Lacey

Physical and emotional pain is inevitable. Suffering is optional. The resistance to the present moment is what causes suffering. "We suffer that we suffer. We get upset about being in pain, angry about dying, sad about waking up sad yet another day. This kind of suffering—which encompasses most of our unhappiness and dissatisfaction—is constructed by the brain. It is made up," says Hanson and Mendius. The brain wants consistency. It learned and stored information, and it wants to efficiently produce the same results. Phil Jackson quotes the famous Zen teacher Suzuki: "Everything changes. Until you accept this, you won't be able to find true equanimity. But to do that means accepting life as it is, not just what you consider the good parts."

Your brain is an amazing tool. Your brain can be thought of as the bouncer at the door alert for trouble or as your best friend. And just like your best friend, you consult him or her for advice, but you don't always take it nor should you. This advice comes from a limited resource based on past experience, social conditioning, and our basic survival instincts.

What is the cure? Hanson and Mendius answer this question with: "For if the brain is the cause of suffering, it can also be the cure." Dethrone the brain and the story it tells you about yourself. Make it the president but not the dictator. Your brain has put itself in charge and worked hard over your lifetime to create personal boundaries in order to more fully protect you. Once a brain creates a boundary, it is much easier to maintain than to allow the boundary to change, grow, or exchange freely without worry from the incoming environmental influences. The more fearful your brain is of losing control of the boundaries it created, the more defensive it becomes towards things that are different.

Your limited brain creates a version of you that it seeks to make more efficient, more independent, and stronger in the face of perceived dangers. Sigmund Freud dubbed this the Ego. In an interview with

An Enlightened Cheerleader

Oprah Winfrey, Eckhart Tolle said, "The Ego wants to be special either by being superior to others or by being more miserable than others." The Ego needs someone or something to beat, wants to be right, and desires to make someone else wrong. It loves to be in conflict with others because it defines itself by being different. This means an enemy or opponent is absolutely essential to the survival of the self. This mentality permeates American society in politics, sports, religion, and war. You need republicans to define a democrat. You need a team to win and a team to lose in every sport. You need Christians to have Muslims. You need an enemy to drop bombs on and destroy. All this happens because we have successfully convinced ourselves that we are right and others are wrong.

Your Ego over time can also create an evil twin and causes conflict within yourself. The evil twin pops up every time you feel judged by others. When you feel judged, your defenses go up, and only with that negative energy can you think of preserving "Me." "Me" has to be right and make the other person wrong in some way. We go to great lengths and hurt many people in our efforts to defend our idea of what is right.

You can't ignore your Ego any more than you can ignore your brain's ability to put itself in charge. But you can decide to have both your brain and your Ego serve your Higher Self. Observe when the Ego is speaking. The Ego develops over our youth from many observations, perceptions, and analysis of our environment and our caretakers. It is like the reflection in the mirror, which isn't real. What we see in the mirror, the reflection, is only what we have decided to show the rest of the world. It in no way encompasses all that we are, and it can be under the interpretation of whoever sees the reflection.

I often hear elder women celebrities say they wish they hadn't been so hard on their twenty-four-year-old self—when they had their beauty and denied it as such. I would say that we should be hard on ourselves,

Wynne Marie Lacey

not for our outer appearances, but by asking the tough questions and getting to know the self fully as a young adult. Don't allow others to direct your thoughts, feelings, and actions. Don't allow the Ego to direct your future self. Get in touch with your Higher Self now, dethrone the Ego and your brain. Do the soul-searching now. Start taking serious responsibility for your self-development.

9

BE YOUR OWN PERSONAL CHEERLEADER

Up to this point in the book, we have talked about Intention, Energy, and Matter. These three components make up Life as we see it on Earth. How do we put this all together and make it useful? To become a Master Reactor, to live at the upper edge of your potential ability, I believe the key is to add Discipline. Discipline will lead you to self-mastery so that you always bring the best of who you are to any situation.

DISCIPLINE + INTENTION + ENERGY
+ MATTER = Master Reactor

You can be your own personal cheerleader. A steadfast, uncritical, enthusiastic supporter of yourself and your goals. Who better than you, since you are the only one with you 100% of the time? You are always

Wynne Marie Lacey

leading yourself, whether you are aware of it or not, so why not lead with positive energy as often as possible?

When you are disciplined, as all cheerleaders are, it means that you are in control of what you can control—you! You will have to renew yourself every day and be committed to doing that the same way you are committed to brushing your teeth or checking Facebook. You will have to take inventory of your intentions, your matter (body and brain) and then know how energy works and how to use it.

First, what are your intentions? How do you get to the meat of who you are and why you are here? As previously stated in the Intentions chapter, I explained how I was unconscious of my intentions to feel the approval of the male species. I had thought becoming the "superior" female would give me the best chances of finding that approval I so desperately needed. At that time in my life, I defined the "superior" female through 80s TV commercials. One commercial you can still find on YouTube is for a perfume called Enjoli. I promise it is worth looking up. It explains *a lot* of how we women think we have to do it all. The commercial started out with a beautiful woman walking in the house from a hard day's work. She was sexy as hell and singing, "I can bring home the bacon, fry it up in a pan, and never let you forget you're a man!" The "bacon" referred to her ability to make her own money and provide for the family. But she was still happy to take care of her household duties like cooking. And finally, she could still be the sex-pot wife that her husband wanted in the bedroom. The lady even pretended to read a book to a child at one point and danced with a pan. She was the ultimate woman, and the most important part that I took away from it was that she looked hot in every scene, specifically for the man.

I am laughing out loud as I write this, and I hope you take the time to look up this commercial and laugh with me. It is an impossible female version to live up to and making intentions to be the "perfect woman"

An Enlightened Cheerleader

in a man's eyes is no longer my intention. I set intentions every day now, but they are different. One intention I currently have is to write in a way that support others, helps them understand themselves, and assists them in fulfilling their own dreams. I have many intentions about my life, and I make sure to review them on a regular basis. As I travel on the journey to enlightenment, my intentions change and grow.

When setting new intentions for yourself, it helps to take inventory of who you have been up to this point in your life and understand how you evolved. Who does your brain say you are? This is your story and worth getting to know really well. It will identify your Ego, patterns, habits, values, and traits. Your brain gives you a set of rules to follow that it has learned for survival in this society. Your brain gives you a sense of individuality and a way to separate yourself from the next person. This happens whether you received countless bouts of praise and trophies or lots of spankings and criticism. Your Ego has learned from everyone else how to be a person. So aren't you really the sum of others? Know that if you don't program your own life, life will program you.

Pick one belief you have about yourself. Where did you get that belief? What evidence do you have that this belief is really true for you? Why does it have to be true for you? Become conscious of the story you tell yourself. Once I realized that the story I was telling myself was partly based on TV commercials from the 80s, it was hilariously funny to me and pretty easy to change my story. "Consciousness is the level of self-awareness, how fully you realize your true self, as opposed to the self you have been trained to see and accept." Schneider continues by saying that when you are self-aware, you will see that it is your exact energetic output that either attracts or repels the desired people and situations in your life.

One of the Foundation Principles of the Institute for Professional Excellence in Coaching (IPEC) [where I received my certificate in life

Wynne Marie Lacey

coaching] is that the world is a perceptual illusion. This means that our interpretation of something is what we perceive as reality. That would also mean that you can always find an interpretation that serves you better. Much of our programming is fear-based and feels more like you have to do something to fit into others' expectations. Replacing the fear-based "have tos" with new programs of passion and "want tos" will open up a new opportunity to live your personal truth, not your ego's limited and fear-based desires.

Lastly, take inventory of your Energy. Find that when you encounter friction, it can be simply a reminder to renew your Energy. The saying, "You are full of hot air," reminds me that I might be working only with the friction in my life, building up heat, but not releasing it and being productive.

One example of how friction was holding me back is in regard to my relationship with my daughter. When she entered kindergarten, we were struggling each morning with what she would wear. She would pick something out, and I would say, "But that doesn't match, Honey—see how you want to match the colors or the patterns?" And she would ask me why? We would argue back and forth and many times she would end up crying.

One morning I hesitated and thought, I don't really have a good answer for her continually questioning why her clothes had to match. I had just been programmed by society that we should match our clothes. Logically, I wanted her to match because I didn't want the teacher to think I didn't care about my daughter's appearance. This is absurd, I thought. I am causing friction and drama between me and my daughter because I see her as an extension of my own Ego. I decided to love my daughter fully and see her as connected to all of me and not just my Ego. I was able to unconditionally love her and allow her space to find what she wants to wear.

An Enlightened Cheerleader

I said, "You can NOT match if that if what you want." And she said that is what she wanted. As I walked out of the room, there was a sense of relief. How wonderful the feeling was. I then asked myself, where did the thought that I have to match come from? Do I have to keep it for me and her? Can I let it go? Is it serving me to have this thought? It did not serve me *in that moment* to have that thought and push it on her. It caused me to not accept my daughter's desires in that moment. I want her to know that I accept her, so I let my thought go that I had to be right and match her clothing for school.

As I walked into my own room, I decided for myself that I *did* want to still match my own clothes. I can have a different thought for me, and we can both be who we want to be in that moment. It was a lovely teaching moment. I see that many of my teaching moments come from my son and daughter, and only because I am in a place of wanting to be in connection with and in total loving energy with my children. What if I wanted that with all people at all times? How do I let others have their thoughts, tell them I accept them, and move on to my own thoughts?

I want to be in total connection to my children. What I do to him or her, I do to myself. If I hurt them, don't understand them, or lead either of them to believe they are unacceptable in my eyes, I do this to myself. I now want to be expanding myself to be connected to other people, even people I don't know, people I used to fear, even people I was told were the enemy or wrong. When I disassociate myself from my ego-based past conditioning, I can ask, why does that have to be true for me? The same way I asked why my daughter has to match her clothes. I don't have a good answer for it.

In the interview with Eckhart Tolle, Oprah refers to the line in his book where he states that this forgetfulness that we are connected to every other being is original sin. "Every act or sinful thing we've heard described is due to a complete disconnection, a lack of understanding

Wynne Marie Lacey

that I am the person or being that I am attempting to violate." "By living through mental definitions of who you are, you desensitize yourself to the deeper aliveness of who you truly are beyond your thoughts." I would add that in an external, appearance-based profession like professional cheerleading, our conceptual identity can become a trap. Time will keep moving, your outer shell will change from youth to old age, and it will devastate those who cannot think differently about themselves.

I can still have different thoughts but completely identify with my daughter's desire to have her own way of expressing herself. I now want her to have her own thoughts, her own experiences of how she presents her "outer shell," and to be accepted for it. She is mismatched on the inside. She has conflicting feelings and wants. So why not express it on the outside with imperfectly perfect clothes? This type of deep connection takes effort on our parts—no doubt about that. Once you make this deep connection, less and less you will seek outside validation. You will be climbing mountains so you can see the world, not so the world can see you. The need to be right and others to be wrong will fall by the wayside as an inner patience with yourself and others begins to develop. You will see that we are all doing the best we can with where we are in our awareness.

As an IPEC-trained Life Coach, my job is to ask questions to clients that slow down their automatic thinking and bring clarity in a way that they can't do for themselves. In her book *Writing to Change the World,* Mary Pipher says, "Either/or thinking is simply not nuanced enough to reflect reality. Business success and economic justice need not be opposites. Women's rights are not anti-family." I would add that being glamorous and sexually seductive to men isn't anti-women's rights either. It has taken me a long time to reach this perspective. If I look at expressing feminine sexuality as an integral part of all that makes us

An Enlightened Cheerleader

female, then I can accept it as an experience that I have had and give others the safe space to have their experience.

Bring awareness to the fact that you are more than you appear to be. It makes you aware that much of what happens to you is unconscious, but you can become conscious. You can wake up. You can take responsibility for who you are and every choice that you make. You can stop judging everything around you and start experiencing it for what it is—*an experience*! That is all you have to call it. *An experience.* And then when you find that every experience is valid, you can consciously digest it for what it is expressing to you because you need to learn it!

This also means that the sum of who you are right now is perfect. Everything that you have experienced was just right for you and for what you needed to learn at that time. That also means that everything that you will experience will be just right for you and for what you need to learn in the future. That finally means that you can experience life in the present moment because that moment is perfect for you.

Open your mind and see that you have all the power within you to make your choices. Get to know your brain and become BFFs. See it as the amazing tool that it is. Understand that it only knows what it has been taught, and that isn't much when you consider the millions of years, billions of people, and trillions of experiences that have graced this planet we call home.

The brain is limited. Your body has limits. The *Invisible Cheerleader* does not have limits. It does not stop creating. Incorporate it consciously and gratefully into your life and see how your outer limits stretch beyond your current imagination. Because our brains are so limited in the way we can comprehend the *Invisible Cheerleader*, it is beneficial to understand ancient wisdom that has stood the test of time when trying to explain it. I personally choose a combination of meditation, life coaching, and the ancient science of Numerology to understand myself.

83

Wynne Marie Lacey

This combination I call Spiritual Logic allows me to become aware of my spiritual self without having to believe any particular story that is part of a religious commitment. You too can be an enlightened being without picking someone else's story to be true for you.

Once you are living in agreement with your whole brain, body, and higher self, you will feel like a butterfly that has emerged from the cocoon. You will know it is only you that has to approve of yourself and enjoy all the parts of yourself. You can be a beautiful *you* from the inside out and show the rest of the world your true purpose because it will be shining from you like the sun. The sun shines because it can not because you ask it to, and the earth benefits from it. But if the earth suddenly spun out of orbit and left this solar system, the sun would continue to shine for itself.

> "Correcting oneself is correcting the whole world. The sun is simply bright. It does not correct anyone. Because it shines, the whole world is full of light. Transforming yourself is a means of giving light to the world" – Annamalai Swami

The butterfly is a great example of "correcting oneself" because it starts out as a caterpillar. The caterpillar is just as valid as any other creature, but it isn't the full story. The caterpillar only reaches its full potential when it literally corrects itself. Clearing out negative beliefs about yourself or others that keep you small and limited corrects yourself. Clearing out emotional attachments to certain people, places, or things because you think they complete you also corrects yourself.

Make no mistake about it. You must clear out a closet before you can put in new stuff. This is so totally true for a human body. This is why a person can think they want to lose weight, but are not be able to do it because they haven't gotten rid of the first thought that takes up the space—the thought that they are not good enough because they aren't

An Enlightened Cheerleader

perfect. Erase thoughts that bind you, and then you will have space for a new thought. That means you have to find out what thoughts you are having about yourself and your limitations in the first place.

Author David Wolfe says, "Everything you have in your life right now is only a duplication of what you subconsciously believe you deserve." That is a pretty eye-opening statement. If your subconscious is full of fear-based thoughts, desires, limiting beliefs, and emotions, then you must clear them away first before you can fit in any new ones. This is not easy. Most people would tell you to think positive or use affirmations. And this comes later. You must first know what you are up against and then clear it out.

This is what I mean by Discipline in the Life Formula. Make sure your new goals are actually yours. You are always headed towards a goal. The question is whose goal is it? You decide what radiant health and positive expression means to you and what you do to experience it. You can dump every thought, feeling, emotion, and action into the Energy category and immediately label it expanding or contracting for you. The outside world is full of contradictions, which fill our minds and bodies with contradictions. Become aware of, sort through the contradictions, and find what is true for yourself.

10

FEMININE FEMINISTS

As you are becoming your own personal cheerleader to reach your highest potential, know that there is enough energy for every living thing on this planet to succeed. It is possible to allow each person to reach for their dreams without feeling in competition with them or feeling you have to be right. Once we support ourselves fully, we can absolutely support other females that we once felt in competition with.

The man-made world creates the false view that we must compete for everything. "The message that competition is appropriate, desirable, required, and even unavoidable is drummed into us from nursery school to graduate school; it is the subtext of every lesson," states Alfie Kohn in *No Contest: The Case Against Competition. Why we Lose in our Race to Win.* There is only one crowned Miss United States, only one winner of every sports championship, only one person who wins the reality TV show, and sadly only one winner of every war. This is man-made

Wynne Marie Lacey

competition—not the natural way of energy in our universe. It is a learned phenomenon and not necessarily what is most natural to a female.

In his book *No Contest,* Alfie Kohn speaks about how competition differs in the man-made world versus the natural world. The man-made world we live in creates competition based on false scarcity, for example, creating a pageant in which there is only one crown. In the natural world, competing with another animal is different because in order to get what you need, you must defeat another because what you want is "scarce by definition". Kohn says not to confuse this with structural competition when the "goal is simply a prized status" where it "usually involves the comparison of several individuals in such a way that only one of them can be the best. The competition itself sets the goal, which is to win; scarcity is thereby created out of nothing."

Structural competition feeds the Egos of our society, as is so evident in the media today. Understanding structural competition for what it is can show you how limiting our Egos can be and how moving towards alignment with a higher creative intelligence will benefit us all. Man-made scarcity is not the natural way of things in our universe, and we could benefit from seeing that there is not just one crown that gets passed around to the lucky and successful. There is a crown for everyone.

Beauty contests in particular don't even require any direct interaction among the contestants when competing. This is the same for competitive cheerleading groups, models competing for the same photo shoot, and dancers auditioning for a limited number of spots on a team. It is the structure of the situation that causes the competition and thereby causes the false, repetitive, deceptive brain messages talked about earlier in this book. Because women are less violent and physical by nature, our competitions tend to be based on comparison rather than

An Enlightened Cheerleader

by combat. We unconsciously believe that if we are a "superior female," there is more of a chance for us to find job success or the prized mate.

Cooperation should first be with the self, working with the energies around you. Once you master yourself, you can then work with others to reach a desired action that produces happiness and fulfillment. Phil Jackson talks about how the Chicago Bulls, led by Michael Jordan, went from a competitive nature that won their first three consecutive world championships to sheer "basketball poetry" when winning their next three championships. Jackson said the "first series of championships transformed the Bulls from an 'I'm great, you're not' team to a 'We're great, they're not' team." But for the second series of championships, the team adopted a broader "life is great" point of view that made it clear to Coach Jackson that, "It wasn't competition per se that was driving the team; it was simply the joy of the game itself." He likens their journey to a dance, "And the only team that could compete against us was ourselves."

Society tells us that status, power, and money are scarce, but that love is also not always available, and we need to earn it. Parents, most likely without meaning to, associate expressing love to their child when he/she accomplishes something that makes the parent proud. Parents show by example that you can't be happy for no reason; there must be a good job, money, vacations, and all sorts of other "prizes" that must be won in life. Today, parents rarely teach children to love themselves simply because they exist on this planet. We think we must motivate our children with competition, or they won't make it in this economy. This sets up a vicious cycle that Kohn describes as, "One has no choice but to be competitive; competition is an unavoidable feature of human life."

Most of you reading this book have every convenience necessary to keep you safe, secure, and never hungry. But most likely you don't feel unconditionally loved, which is just as important as food itself. "If you

Wynne Marie Lacey

want love, then make it," as John Mayer sings in the song *Your Body is a Wonderland*. Love yourself first. Once you love yourself, you can give others that same support. When you are an uncritical, enthusiastic supporter of yourself, you can use that same wonderful energy that helps bring others in your life to a "win." Imagine cheering for yourself and wanting yourself to succeed, then doing the same for others. Kohn says, "Deliberate practice of cooperation is a serious possibility (and) a realistic alternative for our lives." In fact, scientifically, another definition of competition is the "dissipation of energy", while cooperation combines energies and "is the secret of efficient production."

The difference between a sports event and your personal life success is that other women around you don't have to lose for you to win. You can set your own goals and reach them alongside or with the help of others.

> "Many people take the absence of competition to mean that one must be wandering aimlessly, without any goals. But competing simply means that one is working toward a goal in such a way as to prevent others from reaching their goals. This is one approach to getting something done, but (happily) not the only one. Competition need never enter the picture in order for skills to be mastered and displayed, goals set and met." Alfie Kohn

Kohn suggests we ask ourselves, "Do I perform better when I am trying to beat others than when I am working with them or alone?" Studies of competition that he cites show that when children are given the option to cooperate, they chose that over competition. And together the group will have superior performance in classrooms. Kohn goes on to say that after reviewing all the data, the unanimity would astonish most readers and shows that, "We are carefully trained not only to

An Enlightened Cheerleader

compete but to *believe* that a competitive arrangement results in superior performance."

You can choose to lessen your competitive, learned behavior and seek to unearth your more feminine, cooperative nature. Those deceptive brain messages that promote competition, being the best, or having to be better than those around you, can cause us to believe there is only one crown for all the princesses in the room. Some brain messages reiterate over and over that we need approval of others for our outside appearance. Thousands of years of evolution have made us believe that it is not our inner strength that brings us a mate but our ability to attract a male partner through feminine displays of attraction techniques. The desire to attract the male gender is biologically sound and pretending it isn't real for the majority of us is pushing aside a part of our survival instincts. It isn't going anywhere. It is part of a loving, creative, intelligent design that allows our species to reproduce.

Is there a way to honor the historical, evolutionary, and natural reasons females display their beauty, allow them to have these gifts, and then also incorporate the totality of their entire beings? Does it matter whether we are half-naked cheerleaders or professionals in business suits? A current debate around professional cheerleading is the revealing uniforms. It is a symbol to many that women are never fully equal until they put some clothes on. But I would argue to look at other societies, especially in the Middle East, that command women to cover themselves from head to toe. Those women have little to no individual rights and are certainly less respected. So it is not the clothes women wear that define them. We could throw sheets on every woman in America, and it would not help us save the country. The truth is that we have always been equal to men in our influence; we women just haven't completely recognized it yet.

91

Wynne Marie Lacey

So how does society define what is the right amount of clothing to wear? I am not sure it is for society to say, except for those signs that say, "No shirt, no shoes, no service." On a beach in only your bikini, you can certainly get a hotdog vendor to stop and serve you. So it depends on the situation. And in the end, it is up to the individual woman to decide what makes her comfortable in her own skin. There was a time in which I was very comfortable wearing a cheerleading uniform. I am not comfortable wearing one now. And to begrudge beautiful women who can is silly because that is my insecurities being projected onto them.

It might sound odd, but the half-naked professional cheerleading industry is where I believe we can infuse a new Intention into an old movement—the Feminist movement. On RedEye's blog site, a fan posted his feelings about dismissing the Blackhawks Ice Crew: "Pretty girls shoveling snow is no different than pretty girls serving you a beer, or pretty girls waiting your table. Would you rather we lock pretty girls in a basement?"

The original feminism movement was to make women the social equals of men and receive their mutual respect. To do that, these women took a masculine, forceful approach to get their word out. Women in the 60s used angry energy and pushed back at men, justifiably and rightly so. The infamous 1968 Miss America pageant was interrupted by women protesting and throwing their high heels, bras and other female undergarments in a trash can. Such moments helped women's rights to move forward. But I believe they also caused some division and imbalance between women and women, and men and women.

I don't care that men don't wear bras. They don't have the same issues that I do when it comes to keeping my breasts from jumping all over the place. The past feminist movement was valid for using more aggressive, male energy at the time. Some of the big issues they championed were domestic violence, child abuse, daycare, equal pay,

An Enlightened Cheerleader

and reproductive freedoms. We still find women courageously fighting for social change. But I believe we might get farther in our efforts if we use less masculine energy and move towards using feminine energy.

Today's women may not think of themselves as feminists when women of the past were fighting for the right to vote and receive fair employment practices. But if feminism truly means freedom to practice personal self-development, then I believe we are collectively doing that. So to me it seems fitting that the thousands who have been, currently are, or aspiring to be professional cheerleaders can lead a new kind of feminist movement—the Feminine Feminist. Let's keep our bras on! And bling it if you want!

This new Feminine Feminist would champion beauty as one of the many gifts that human beings receive, and she would not blame the striving for exceptional beauty as one of the downfalls of women. We can celebrate that a woman can be beautiful and do meaningful things with her life. Perhaps a stated feminist goal could be to appreciate beauty's magnificence and allow beautiful women their beauty as an act of personal liberation. The pursuit of beauty would become more self-directed and less about getting validation from others because of being more attractive than another.

Professional cheerleaders as well as all women have a certain power in being able to attract the attention of many men. Let's add to our power. Not just through our ability to attract men but to see ourselves as capable individuals who can do anything we set our minds to. And it can be a supportive role to the world but with deeper meaning. Women can lead with their feminine energies. We can become our own food-chain of energy, share the healthiest opportunities amongst our common gender, and do more for humanity.

Statistics show that women have higher rates of education and purchasing power right now. Why worry so much about getting ahead

93

Wynne Marie Lacey

in male-patterned businesses when we have all the freedom in the world to cooperate and nurture within our society? I think it feels unnatural to women to be leaders in the form of "power over others." Not because we are taught that, but because it really doesn't make sense as a way for human beings to flourish.

When you are the all-powerful CEO of a company, it is your agenda that is being pushed out of the thousands of employees that work for you. That isn't natural, do you think? What woman looks around and says, "I want all these people to do what I say and make me lots of money!?" There is no shame in thinking about others, wanting true equality for all persons, and sharing resources without dominating others. I think those are qualities that we can persuade our male counterparts to see as very valuable in themselves. Kohn quotes linguist Robin Lakoff:

> "Although in many ways the typical feminine style doesn't get you what you want, nevertheless it's exceedingly valuable. It would be a pity if it were to vanish. The alternative, the male style, has so many bad aspects of its own that nobody is advised to acquire it... Anything that allows the other person to have room is in itself a good thing, something that suggests cooperation."

If equality is really just about giving women the same choices as men, then perhaps we could lead men to choose more like a woman. We could set examples of how cooperation and supporting a group can be just as rewarding as competition. I know many women I believe to be leaders. They aren't named to the Forbes 100 List and don't make a lot of money in business. Kohn states, "The fact that women's values have tended to clash with the demands of competitive, male-dominated institutions does not mean that the former ought to adjust to fit the latter." Kohn quotes Lakoff again:

An Enlightened Cheerleader

"[It's not] that there is something wrong with women… [but] that there is something wrong with this definition of success and that there is something right with women's inability to accommodate this definition… It no longer seems appropriate to rout out success anxiety and replace it with acceptance of the masculine rules of the game. Rather, women now need to focus on affirming the structures and values they bring to the question of competition versus relationships and start reconstructing institutions according to what women know."

Feminine energy stirs from deep within the core of us. Ask any woman who birthed a child. We can build up the balance of female desire to take care of everything in the home and to make us feel safe and supported. We can look deep within ourselves to let go of the past idea of what our role should have been and wake up to the commitment of our roles in the future. The old roles for masculine dominance no longer work for this planet. We can help transition from "having to be right" to starting to open up the compassionate side of the feminine energy. Feminine energy contains fluidity, care, patience, perseverance, strength beyond physical understanding, empathy, multi-perspective, ancient knowledge, and the capacity of all the senses. We can make a conscious choice to start leading with our more natural feminine energies.

11

CARPE DIEM

arpe Diem is a famous expression meaning to enjoy, make use of, or to "Seize the Day." I use it to remind myself of the formula D + I + E + M (Discipline, Intention, Energy, Matter) and to include all four pieces as I go through my day. I want to enjoy, make use of, and seize each day with the discipline I need to be aware of my intentions, focus my anabolic energy, and take care of the only body I have for this whole lifetime.

I consider myself a practicing Feminine Feminist who is working towards becoming an Enlightened Cheerleader. I am free-thinking, loving, open-minded, tolerant, and an uncritically enthusiastic supporter of each one of you reading this book. I believe it is your individual right to search for meaning in your life no matter how you choose to do it. I love the age-old cheer, "We got spirit, yes we do, we got spirit, how 'bout you?!" And I find spirit to be a universal <u>energy</u> present individually in all living things.

Wynne Marie Lacey

Enlightening my "self" through the cheerleader journey turned out to be very appropriate for me. Spirit appears so much around the cheerleading industry. I was drawn to the industry for the potential that it stood for and stay in it for the future potential that it holds. A potential that when opened will move quickly through my peers and resonate with many people who came to be cheerleaders in hopes of finding what was missing in their lives. If we can move past our Egos, I know we can make a statement about women, femininity, and our worth to mankind and the planet.

In chapter two, I wrote about the challenges that I saw for professional cheerleaders which I consider challenges for most women these days in our society. The first challenge was how we tend to lose our personal identity. When we take steps towards enlightenment, we begin to see that we have the power to define ourselves. Hanson and Mendius tell us, "It's a general moral principle that the more power you have over someone, the greater your duty is to use that power benevolently. Well, who is the one person in the world you have the greatest power over? It's your future self. You hold that life in your hands, and what it will be depends on how you care for it."

The second challenge discussed in chapter two is losing contact with our personal values. As we travel towards enlightenment, we start to see ourselves as a soul with a body, and we place much more importance on our inner development. The Ego goes from the driver's seat to the passenger's seat. We start believing in ourselves *before* others see it. And it doesn't matter if others don't acknowledge it in us. We see ourselves as unique, offering purpose and harmony to this planet. If you were a replica of someone else here, what would be your purpose? Believe that you deserve to live out your life in your way. Every time you act, ask if it is from some external cue about what others think of you or an internal cue coming from your heart's desire?

An Enlightened Cheerleader

The third challenge from chapter two is having too much emphasis placed on the outer appearance. As we journey towards enlightenment, two things will happen. One, we will start to see beauty where we didn't see it before. We will appreciate all types of women, like we appreciate the few days we have to see a flower blooming in the spring. Second, we will no longer feel threatened by youthful beauty in others because we will see beauty in a different way. It is a gift among many gifts, and it is temporary just like everything else on the planet. And because each person has come here to experience their body through their soul-eyes, we will look deeper, past the exterior appearance.

The fourth challenge mentioned in chapter two is experiencing unnatural, competitive situations with other females. As we travel towards enlightenment, we see that we don't have to be the "superior female." Women have *always* been equal to men. For example, women not being allowed to vote is not a *truth*. Women are certainly physically and mentally capable of voting, and they always were. It took a female to realize it and to stand up and say it. Someone just had to become aware of it, question what was true in the moment, and seek the deeper truth within herself. Then another and another found this same *truth*, and enough awareness was brought to our society to tip the scales from *true* to *truth*. So now it is both true and the truth that women vote in this country, and it is in harmony with society. The *truth* never changed, it just had to be acknowledged and then someone had to *take action*.

The fifth and last challenge discussed in chapter two is how cheerleaders have to produce a happy face in all situations. As we travel towards enlightenment, we can still be at peace through unhappy times because we will see unpleasant moments as a perfect opportunity to savor the lesson we are learning and observe the way it leads us to a happier moment. The prediction that we will be happy and at peace when we have this or achieve that no longer defines our ability to be

99

happy. An enlightened cheerleader is less concerned about being happy and more concerned about being present in the moment. Because when you are consciously aware in the present moment, you are able to filter out past internal blocks and any future distractions. The present "you" is the best "you" because it's the real "you". There is no better moment in your life than this moment because it is the only moment you have.

When we let go of the need to control and create our lives, we also let go of frustration. Humans don't actually create anything new out of nothing—ever. I am not telling you anything new; many others already know this and share it with me through language and personal interpretation. Everything that will ever be discovered, understood, or produced already exists on some level and did so before we probably first set foot on this planet. And that is truly a gift, if you think about it. Because when everything you could possibly ever need has been provided to you, you get to play and experience life!

Everything is meant to be respected and shared. So how do we feel special when we aren't? How do we feel validated, accomplished, creative, and productive simply through our own human efforts? How do we stay creators of man-made "things" while acknowledging a larger, more powerful creative process of which we are a small part?

The answer is to be in sync with the *Invisible Cheerleader*. Finding your purpose in relation to this world is key to feeling less like a fraud and more like the God-energy that brought you into being. And we do this first with mental energy. Thoughts. Observations. Experience. Choosing. Conscious awareness. All of the true, lasting wisdom of our species comes from those who quieted their minds, observed their surroundings, and shared their thoughts peacefully with others.

But finding everlasting wisdom wasn't the last thing they did, either. They *took action*. Masters like Jesus did the work *after* being enlightened. Stories of Jesus weren't just about talking the talk; he

An Enlightened Cheerleader

walked the walk. He integrated himself into other's lives and embodied what he preached. And Jesus didn't judge others. He knew we are all here to love each other and create harmony in what we *do*. St. Francis of Assisi is another great example of this. His famous saying, "Preach the gospel, and when necessary, use words," is about taking the actions that an enlightened person would take, not just talking about them.

Being an Enlightened Cheerleader doesn't mean we sit around all day and meditate. Cheerleaders are the doers of society and the busiest females I know! We interact differently. We create harmony. We create cooperation. We support our teams. And we do it when it is really hard, like when our sports teams are losing. We are the ones who think we can do it no matter what.

And now it is up to us cheerleaders to spread the love! Carpe Diem!

CREED OF AN ENLIGHTENED CHEERLEADER

One who knows that pain is inevitable, but suffering is optional. Joy is also inevitable, and it is up to us to savor our happy moments. We are at the cause of our life, not just the effect.

One who knows that the road to self-mastery begins with getting to know the self, first. Each of us is greater and wiser than we appear to be.

One who knows that where she is going doesn't have to be based on where she has been. The truth is that there is no right or wrong, just what I have been taught. There are no mistakes, just mis-interpretations.

One who's true nature is a Soul that has a body and an ego to use in this lifetime. She is in service to a higher spirit and does not let her ego lead her journey.

One who knows that love always triumphs over fear. There is no winning or losing, only gaining.

One who knows that we are subject to Universal Laws that are in place for us to reach our highest potential. We are wired not to just survive, but thrive.

One who lives in a competitive world but chooses cooperation in all that she pursues. We offer passion, process, and possibilities to anyone who wants them.

One who takes action and uses her "pom-pom" waving skills to get the world's attention and raise the standards of the human race.

REFERENCES

1) Bolohan, Scott, "Lose the Ice Crew," *RedEye* (blog), April 23, 2013, http://www.redeyechicago.com/sports/ct-red-0424-bolohan-column-20130423,0,470207.story.

2) Crawford-Carnegie, Michele Mickey. *Alumni Cheerleaders,* 2013, http://www.alumnicheerleaders.com.

3) Dyer, Wayne. *The Power of Intention. Learning to Co-create Your World Your Way.* California: Hay House, Inc., 2004.

4) Godman, David. *Living by the Words of Bhagavan.* India: Annamalai Swami Ashram, 1994.

5) Hanson, Rick and Richard Mendius, MD. *Buddha's Brain- The Practical Neuroscience of Happiness, Love and Wisdom.* California: New Harbinger Publications, 2009.

6) Hochman, David. "Michael J. Fox," *AARP Magazine,* April/May 2013, 38-39.

7) Huie, Johnathan Lockwood. *Positive Affirmations,* 2013 http://www.johnathanlockwoodhuie.com.

8) Jackson, Phil and Hugh Delehanty. *Eleven Rings – The Soul of Success*. New York: The Penguin Group, 2013.

9) Kohn, Alfie. *No Contest: The Case Against Competition. Why we Lose in Our Race to Win*. New York: Houghton Mifflin Company, 1992.

10) Mayer, John. *Room for Squares*. Sony Music Entertainment, 2001.

11) Pielou, E.C. *The Energy of Nature*. Chicago: University of Chicago Press, 2001.

12) Pipher, Mary. *Writing to Change the World*. New York: The Penguin Group, 2007.

13) Schneider, Bruce D. *Energy Leadership: Transforming your Workplace and Your Life from the Core*. New Jersey: John Wiley & Sons, 2008.

14) Schneider, Bruce D. *Life and Leadership Potentials Training Workbook*. New Jersey: Institute for the Professional Excellence in Coaching, 2009.

15) Schucman, Helen, Dr. *A Course in Miracles*. Mill Valley, CA: Foundation for Inner Peace, 2010.

16) Schwartz, Jeffrey and Rebecca Gladding. *You are not Your Brain*. New York: The Penguin Group, 2011.

17) Vultaggio, Maria. "Is Kelsey Williams Fat? Claire Crawford Blogs NBA Cheerleader Is 'Too Chunky" To Wear Oklahoma City Thunder Uniform," *International Business Times*, April 28, 2013. http://www.ibtimes.com/kelsey-williams-fat-claire-crawford-blogs-nba-cheerleader-too-chunky-wear-oklahoma-city-thunder.

18) Watts, Alan. *Oriental Philosophy*. Electronic University, 2011.

19) *Wikipedia*, s. v. "Galileo Affair," last modified 2008, http://en.wikipedia.org/wiki/Galileo_affair.

20) Winfrey, Oprah. "Oprah Talks to Eckhart Tolle," *The Oprah Magazine*, May 2008.

21) Wolfe, David. *The Sunfood Diet Success System*. Berkeley: North Atlantic Books, 2009.

CPSIA information can be obtained at www.ICGtesting.com
Printed in the USA
LVOW13s0352170114

369704LV00001B/76/P